OFFIC AT RISK

HOW TO IDENTIFY AND COPE WITH STRESS

Dennis L. Conroy, Ph.D.
St. Paul Police Department

Kären M. Hess, Ph.D.
Normandale Community College

1992

CUSTOM PUBLISHING COMPANY

1590 Lotus Road
Placerville, California 95667
916 626-1260

Your Partner in Education
With
"QUALITY TEXTS AT FAIR PRICES"

OFFICERS AT RISK:
How to Identify
and Cope With Stress

Copyright © 1992 by Custom Publishing Company

Developmental Editor - Derald D. Hunt

Library of Congress Catalog Number: 91-73969

ISBN 0-942728-48-3 Paper Text Edition

Printed in the United States of America

DEDICATION

To those officers who hurt and can't talk about it—so they at least will know that other officers feel the same.

And especially to Captain Rocky Winger (1941-1990), one of the best people in the world, but who truly paid a price.

D.L.C.

About the Authors . . .

Dennis L. Conroy, Ph.D.

Dennis L. Conroy is a Sergeant with the St. Paul, Minnesota Police department and is currently assigned as a juvenile investigator. He has been a police officer for over 20 years. He has worked as a patrol officer, patrol supervisor, vice-narcotics investigator, trainer, and Employee Assistance Program director. Dr. Conroy has a Ph.D. in Clinical Psychology and conducts a psychology practice and consulting business.

Kären M. Hess enjoys national recognition as an author and a teacher of law enforcement communication. She has authored or coauthored more than 30 books. She has lectured extensively in writing, communications, and management. She is President of the Institute for Professional Development, Bloomington, Minnesota. Dr. Hess earned her Ph.D. from the University of Minnesota

Kären M. Hess, Ph.D.

CONTENTS

Foreword   vii
Acknowledgments   ix
Introduction   xi

PART I: OVERVIEW OF OFFICERS AND STRESS   1
  1. The Price Police Officers Pay   3
  2. The Price Correctional Officers Pay   13
  3. A Close-Up View of Stress   23
  4. Officers as Victims   35
  5. Post-Traumatic Stress Disorder   55

PART II: INDIVIDUAL MEANINGS   79
  6. Loss of Innocence   81
  7. Cynicism   95
  8. Loneliness   107
  9. Isolation   119
 10. Constricted and Inappropriate Affect   131
 11. Importance of the Police-Corrections Family   141

PART III: IMPLICATIONS   153
 12. Meanings for Individual Officers   155
 13. Meanings for Officers' Families   165
 14. Administrative Meanings   177
 15. Training and Supervision Issues   187
 16. Counseling Applications   197

PART IV: PROGRAMS TO REDUCE BURNOUT   207
 17. Preventing Personal Burnout   209
 18. Organizational Stress Management   231

  Epilogue   251
  Appendix   253
  Glossary   255
  Index   261

FOREWORD

Understanding that police and correctional officers are secondary victims of stress is usually dismissed by those who are uninformed about these professions. The general public fails to comprehend, or worse yet, minimizes what types of stress these officers continually face. Therefore, resources that may diminish the severity of the impact on these victims are usually not provided by the community.

Law enforcement officers may feel they are literally fighting a war. Correctional officers may feel as if they are involved in a combat situation. Both groups sense little support or empathy for their effort, bravery, and dedication to the cause.

Dr. Conroy and Dr. Hess have together compiled a detailed manuscript indispensable for anyone who wants to gain an understanding of the realities of police and corrections work. The associated stressors affect the lives of officers and those people they are sworn to protect.

Officers at Risk should be on the priority reading list for anyone involved or associated with law enforcement or corrections work. Law enforcement and corrections administrators, elected officials, wives, family, friends, the press, and especially officers themselves, should consider this book "must reading."

This work cites many excellent descriptions and examples of how the stress process takes place. The authors describe the stages and emotions through which most law enforcement and correctional personnel move. Many times victims themselves may not realize they are participating in a negative, emotional scenario. Officers cannot walk away from the conflict or the trauma which they must routinely handle. They confront so many traumatic incidents that they may be unaware of negative changes in their own lives.

I must thank Drs. Conroy and Hess for writing a book which may help change the attitudes of those people who can make a difference in the field, such as police and corrections administrators, psychologists, social workers, teachers, community leaders, as well as the officers and their families. As a result of that cognitive awareness, new processes can be initiated to cope with and mitigate the stress.

The last point which I feel must be made is that every law enforcement and correctional officer is at risk. Many are not aware of the risk until negative changes have occurred and they feel trapped with no apparent exit.

If you feel that you have to pick one book on police and correctional officer stress, I believe *Officers at Risk* is your book.

Congratulations to Conroy and Hess for this important, informative, and well-researched piece of work.

John J. Millner
Chief of Police
Elmhurst, Illinois

ACKNOWLEDGMENTS

A sincere thank you to Christine for her careful data entry and valuable editorial contributions. A heartfelt thanks to Ann for her understanding and patience, to Gwen for her invaluable input, and to Mike for the fishing trips he gave up while the book was being written.

Sergeant *Dennis L. Conroy*

<><>

CREDITS

Photographs by
Dennis Conroy
J. Scott Harr

Research by
Edith Kromer
Pam Reirson

Cartoon Illustrations by
Joe Guy

INTRODUCTION

Officers at Risk is for anyone affected by the stress of working in law enforcement or corrections. It is meant for individual officers, their supervisors and managers, their families, and even for those who would like to become police or correctional officers.

The terms *police, police officer,* and *police work,* as used in this text, are meant in their more generic sense. For example, officers working as sheriff's deputies, state police, metropolitan police, and highway patrol officers are exposed to many, if not all, of the stress factors discussed here. This book is intended for these officers as well as municipal (city) police officers.

The information in this book is crucial for chaplains and others providing counseling to officers, their spouses and families, so they are aware of the impact a law enforcement or correctional career has on those involved—and how that impact affects counseling.

This text emphasizes the importance of information and understanding for officers and their families on how to deal with the stress of a law enforcement or corrections career. It presents an up-to-date look at the *real meanings of stress* for those who deal with crime and criminals daily—and the price they pay to do so.

Officers at Risk is based on the research (described in the Appendix) of Dr. Dennis L. Conroy and on his twenty years' experience as a police officer, clinical experience with law enforcement and correctional officers, and experience as a trainer of both.

PART I begins by looking at the price police officers (Chapter 1) and correctional officers (Chapter 2) are paying due to job stress. This is followed by a close-up view of stress

(Chapter 3), officer "victimization" (Chapter 4), and post-traumatic stress disorder (Chapter 5).

This broad overview of stress, trauma, and change as it relates to police and correctional officers, is followed by an in-depth discussion of *meanings* for these officers, that is, what it *means* to be a cop or a prison guard.

PART II is a more detailed look at some "prices" paid by those who become police and correctional officers: a loss of innocence (Chapter 6), cynicism and negativism (Chapter 7), loneliness and sadness (Chapter 8), isolation (Chapter 9), and a constricted and inappropriate affect (Chapter 10). Accompanying these "prices" is the inevitable closing of ranks of the occupational family (Chapter 11).

Although each of these "prices" are discussed in separate chapters, they seldom occur in isolation or in their "pure" state. The overlap found in some examples underscores the complexity as well as the extensive effects of stress.

PART III discusses the implications of the changes police and correctional officers go through and the emotional battles they wage. It looks at meanings for individual officers (Chapter 12), for their families (Chapter 13), for police departments and prisons (Chapter 14), for those involved in training and supervision (Chapter 15), and for counselors who deal with these officers (Chapter 16).

PART IV presents plans to prevent individual burnout (Chapter 17) and many suggestions to prevent organizational or institutional burnout (Chapter 18).

PART I

AN OVERVIEW OF
OFFICERS AND STRESS

Statistics fully verify that police and correctional officers are at great risk from the effects of stress. Few statistics are cited in this book, however, because for those officers who are paying or have paid the price, it's the tears that count.

Officers at Risk begins by looking at some tremendous "prices" individual officers have paid as the result of being a cop (Chapter 1) or a prison guard (Chapter 2).

Since both law enforcement and corrections are extremely stressful occupations, the *concept* of stress is the focus of Chapter 3. Stress is defined and models of stress are discussed, as are the stages of change officers typically experience. The different stressors of each stage of a typical police and corrections career are described—with explanations of the effect on the individual.

Chapter 4 highlights current theories of "victimization," including the emotional and cognitive stages victims experience. This chapter describes not only how officers deal with victims and those who victimize, but also how these officers themselves **become** victims.

Chapter 5 discusses post-traumatic stress disorder and shows how officers' involvement with trauma takes a toll on their personal and professional lives. Comparisons are made between the experiences of police and correctional officers and the combat experiences of Vietnam veterans. Diagnostic criteria for post-traumatic stress disorder are discussed and related to police and correctional officers.

Just wait . . . they're still new.

Chapter 1

THE PRICE
POLICE OFFICERS
PAY

You can talk all you want about what it looks like, what ya see, a dead kid laying in the street who's just been run over by a garbage truck, and that sticks in your mind for the rest of your life. Or a little kid that I carried out of a burning house, you work your ass off to save, and he dies anyway. Those things don't leave ya. They scar your mind and affect your life.*

Police officers change. Many officers feel that police work, by its very nature, affects their entire being. After working on the job for a few years, you may wonder what has happened, in what ways you have changed, and, most importantly, how you have ended up being as you are:

I was one of the best, I was one of the nicest, one of the most trustworthy, most sincere, most honest, most caring human beings you ever met in your whole life. But now, all I know is I ain't what I was. I've become something totally different than what I was brought up by my mom and dad to be.

Another officer put it this way:

---

*Unless otherwise noted, all quotations are from the research of Dennis L. Conroy, PhD.

3

I was scared of myself. I was scared of the way I looked at myself, the way I acted, what I was doing. I didn't like it. I can't say that I didn't like all of it. Some of it was okay, but it just got real scary. I mean, everything that I did turned into a real life-threatening situation. I put myself in those situations. I don't know what it was. I was just doing crazy things.

When we first started working alone in cars, I used to purposely be the first one in to calls. We weren't supposed to go in alone, but I figured I could do anything. I didn't care if it was a fight, a gun call, or a shooting.

Why? What changes people who become police officers?

WHY PREVIOUS STUDIES FAILED

For years officers have been pinched, poked, and prodded by researchers to see how they jumped. Researchers have come to officers and said, "These things are important. Tell me which is the most important." Or, "These things cause stress. Tell me which causes the most stress." Officers have been rated, scaled, chosen, and listed until it seems meaningless to the individual officer. Yet few have asked what should be the first and most important question, "What is important to *you*?" In other words, "What does this really *mean*? How does this affect *your* life?"

Until now police officers have been most often "studied" like laboratory animals. Their world has been described in the sterile terms of quantitative research by sociologists, psychologists, social workers, and other researchers, but not by police officers themselves. I have listened to these officers speak from the heart, describing what is most important to them, how they are affected, and what they see as the real meanings of police work.

Many officers find they change after entering law enforcement—often quite dramatically:

For me it was a transition—from total innocence and being totally naive. I changed a lot. I'm not sure I gave up anything. I lost some things, but I'm not sure I gave them up. I lost my humanity. I don't know how else to describe it.

Probably a greater loss than losing my humanity, is to know that it's not there and saying, "That's okay, I don't want it." That's a bigger loss 'cause to want it makes you soft and vulnerable–and I don't want to be vulnerable anymore.

WHAT THE LITERATURE SAYS

Interestingly, current literature deals with almost every aspect of law enforcement work *except* what stress for officers is *really* like. You'll find books, for example, about enforcement tactics, community relations, police divorce, alcohol abuse, and suicide rates, to name a few. Literature about "officer stress," however, is almost exclusively a collection of tables, statistics, and cause/effect discussions.

This literature identifies "stressors," ranks their importance, and measures their effects on the individual and the organization (e.g. use of sick leave and job performance). These effects have been labeled "stress." However, they deal with cause and effect–not meanings.

LAW ENFORCEMENT WORK–HOW STRESSFUL?

The National Institute for Occupational Safety and Health ranks police work in the top third of 130 "high stress" professions (Pelletier, 1984). Your career is a series of ups and downs. As you continue through each work day, you are constantly subjected to different types of stress.

A contributing factor to this overall stress is the necessity to shift gears abruptly–to go from a rape to a barking dog complaint. It becomes difficult to handle all calls as they should be handled because of the extreme variance in importance and the differing levels of emotional intensity:

You go and handle a call where you put the kid in a shelter because he's been sodomized by his dad for half his life and he's traumatized, and his mom's traumatized, and the next call ya get is some guy bitching because his parking spot is screwed up in front of his house. You want to say, "Take your petty problems and stick them up your ass." But you can't do that because the people downtown say so.

Certainly police work is not always hazardous, but often you have either just captured a criminal or are looking for one. You may have either recently experienced a physical assault or must be prepared for one in the near future. And you ride for many hours a day, listening to reports over the radio of attacks, rapes, burglaries, domestic assaults, and aggression against fellow officers, interspersed with people locked out of their homes or cars, or raccoons up chimneys.

In addition, you carry around a belt loaded with fifteen to twenty pounds of armament and defense equipment and wear a bulletproof vest (all terribly uncomfortable). This is oppressive and tends to create an environment of anticipation of violence and, on some level, an obsession with personal vulnerability. You are keenly aware that during a totally boring "dogwatch," a life-threatening situation might be just a moment away.

THE PRICE OF CONSTANT VIGILANCE

You are constantly reminded of the occupational dangers through officer safety training encouraging you to be ever vigilant. This training is obviously essential for your safety. However, the price you pay is high for having to be constantly alert for someone who may want to injure or kill you for little or no apparent reason. The price of this vigilance is a general inability to relax while working.

This inability to relax can extend beyond your work to your home life and leads to a particularly distrustful world view:

I think that even carries over into my personal life, that lack of trust. I can't say I distrust my friends, but when they're telling stories about something that happened to them, I always think, "Well, yah, there's more to it than that." I don't accept too much on face value anymore.

Another officer expressed similar feelings:

Instead of just being suspicious of a suspect in a crime, you become suspicious that your wife is being unfaithful to you, that your brother is a sex pervert, that other cops are drug addicts.

One positive side of police stress is the excitement. The incredible feeling when the pulse quickens, the senses keen, and all your energy focuses on crisis can translate into status for you: "The more stress you're put under, the more exciting the job is—the more difficult or the more prestige the assignment held, the more fun, the more you wanted it."

OVERALL EFFECTS OF STRESS

The effect of stress on personal functioning has been and still is the subject of considerable research and public interest. Such research has been quantitative and focused on identifying stressors and measuring stress in police officers.

Swanton (1980), for example, discussed the causes and results of stress among police officers. Among identified causes were administrative stress originating in excessive paperwork and a perceived lack of support from superior officers; stress from job conflicts (e.g., when a criminal is released through a "legal technicality"); stress from public criticism and from constant exposure to value systems and lifestyles contrary to their own.

Among the effects identified were excessive drinking, promiscuity, reclusiveness, loss of interest in work, depression, physical ailments, and suicide.

- **Excessive drinking and promiscuity:** "There was booze and sex and violence and macho and all that, but there wasn't much place for intimacy. Just rah, rah, macho, tough talk, comradery amongst the other cops."

- **Reclusiveness:** "I just want to get as far away as I can and live with the scorpions."

- **Loss of interest in work:** "I always really wanted to be a cop. I didn't want just a job. I wanted it to be something really special, something that I really like. Some people go to their jobs, and they hate their work and look forward to the weekends and getting off. I didn't want that. I loved my job, but that has changed in the last year and a half."

- **Depression:** "I hate my job. I can't stand it. I hate the city. I hate the chief. I hate the men. I never used to be that way. It's getting so I don't want to come to work anymore. I could have called in sick today and nothing would have changed, not a thing. And it wouldn't have mattered, and tomorrow it wouldn't matter, and the next day and ten years from now. And I mean it wouldn't matter."

- **Stress-related physical ailments:** "I've had some medical problems and that was directly, according to what the doctor said, was job related. I had a couple of heart attacks and I had to have open heart surgery. They said it was because of the stress of the job."

- **Suicide:** "I think it [suicide] is a really viable alternative. Just leave when you've had enough and you don't want to participate anymore–just a good way to leave. And of course, if you plan it properly it looks more like an accident than a suicide. And that lets the family and everybody off the hook, doubles your insurance, and makes a nice little package."

OTHER REACTIONS TO STRESS

Henderson (1981), identified two major reactions of police to stress: withdrawal (passive) and aggression (active). He also identified three major categories of *stress defense mechanisms*:

Deception, or hiding the perception of the threat.

Substitution, or replacing stressful with non-stressful or less stressful goals.

Avoidance, or removing oneself from the stress.

He noted that when defense mechanisms such as repression, projection, and rationalization are used to cope with stress, maladaptive behavior can result in depression, cynicism, alienation, loneliness, and despair.

One officer described his choice of coping mechanisms when he said:

> I would drink over a lot of stuff rather than talk about it, drink it away. You'd drink over it, you would have sex over it, you could party over it, you could buy toys, you could work a lot. You could do a lot of things rather than face your feelings. I did most of those things rather than face my feelings.

Many things some officers perceive as stressful, others consider to be simply part of the job. For example, prosecuting attorneys are often reluctant to prosecute offenders for assaulting a police officer, even though a similar offense against a citizen is almost guaranteed a prosecution. You are told that to be spit on is simply part of the job and that you must accept such degradation as a "professional hazard."

This is stressful because you know through experience that neither the judge nor the prosecutor would consider an assault simply a part of their job, nor would they accept being spit on as a "professional hazard." In such cases, it seems you are being held to unreasonable standards.

THE PROCESS OF CHANGE FOR OFFICERS

The price you pay to be a police officer is high. The changes brought about within the world of individual officers are varied, but they are initially negative and generally

damaging to the individual. This way of life includes loneliness, cynicism, sadness, isolation, and a strong identification
with the police culture.

Adapting to police work is a *process*. You begin with a
naive view of law enforcement. You move from this view
through the stage of being-in-the-world as police officers-
victims. You ultimately move through this stage to an adjustment in which you understand the importance of your work,
but are no longer attached to only the police culture.

During this process you are exposed to a significant amount
of potential stressors. Your world view changes, the perception of the event changes, and your responses can be very
different during different parts of your career.

For example, initially you may perceive the administration
as stress producing. As you move through the professional
maturing process, you are likely to come to the realization that
you have little control over the administration's actions. With
this realization, you can reassess the situation and accept it as
simply annoying rather than as critical to your well being.

"Shouldn't someone here be on my side?"

REFERENCES

Henderson, G. (1981). "Police Need People." In G. Henderson (Ed.), *Police Human Relations,* (pp.149-169). Springfield: Charles C. Thomas.

Pelletier, K. (1984). *Healthy People in Unhealthy Places: Stress and Fitness at Work.* New York: Delacorte Press.

Swanton, B. "Stress in the Police Service." *Federal Police Journal.* VI, N7 (April 1980), pp. 9, 20-26, 31.

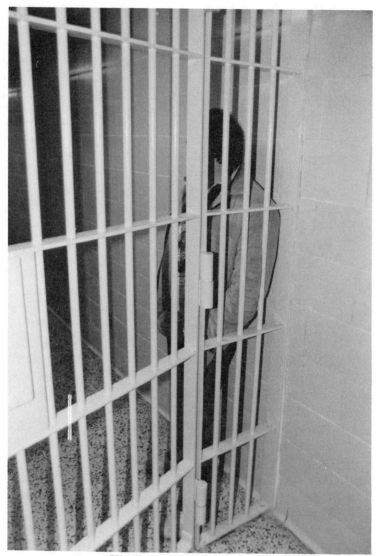

The bars work both ways.

Chapter 2

THE PRICE
CORRECTIONAL OFFICERS
PAY

This past year I found myself in a position where it was snowballing. Everything was looking lousy to me. My job was crap, my relationship was crap, my relationship with my friends was crap. I was the rock of Gibraltar and things were falling apart around me, and I had nowhere to turn. I was looking for something to grasp a hold of, but I didn't find it, so I took a big nose dive.

Some differences are important between correctional officers and police officers. Correctional officers:

- Deal more with people who are in custody.
- Have limited contact with crime victims.
- Are generally unarmed.
- Do not usually have to deal with the weather.

Such differences, however, are minor compared to the tremendous similarities between the two occupations.

STRESS SIMILARITIES

Many stressors affecting police officers are the same for correctional officers. Both are often in an antagonistic role

with the population they serve. Both may sometimes feel
unsupported by the administration they work for. And both
see little success in reaching their assigned goal. You see the
same inmates coming back time after time for the same
offense, some spending the majority of their adult lives in
prison—in small doses.

While correctional officers do not deal with the victims as
police officers do, they do deal with the victimization because
every time they see an inmate return, they know that the
system has failed again.

STEREOTYPING

Correctional officers are also stereotyped. Both correctional and police officers are often portrayed as large males
with more muscles than brains who are inefficient, not only
through their stupidity, but also through intentional dishon-
esty. Cartoons or articles about "crooked guards" or "crooked cops" are frequent.

A few superficial changes have occurred. For example, the
word *pig* has gone out of fashion to refer to police officers,
and prison guards are now referred to as *correctional counselors*. But in each case the job remains much the same. You
deal with the same population as before and use many of the
same methods to get the job done. The methods have
become more "humane" for both professions, but the public
image of the job is the same. Police officers are accused of
framing inmates to get them into prison, and correctional
officers are accused of brutalizing them and granting special
favors to those inmates with "pull."

SURVIVAL CHANGES

Like police officers, correctional officers indicate that their
work has changed them and they have paid a large price as a
result.

Many correctional officers describe these changes as necessary to survive, but also as unanticipated and as not helpful in non-work relationships. The changes frequently involve a loss of naivety, a new awareness of the world, loss of the ability to trust, development of a cynical outlook, and strained relationships with your friends and spouse.

LOSS OF INNOCENCE

The first change seems to be a loss of innocence. Many persons enter the corrections field unaware of the extent to which crimes and criminals pervade our society:

I came in a little naive. Now that I think back, I came in here a happy-go-lucky, love everybody, you know, sunshine, rosy kind of a guy. I was trusting. I was quite candid, and I got trampled on big time. I befriended people that I thought would be my friends forever, and that wasn't the case.

Another correctional officer described similar changes:

I basically grew up in a white, middle-class community, and so I really didn't have that much to do with minorities or crime. I think once I got out of high school and got out of college and came here it was kind of disheartening to see how bad people could be.

Some of my values, my beliefs about people changed. I think there's a tendency after you work here to say, "Don't give anyone the benefit of the doubt. They're just looking for something from you."

Many correctional officers become less trusting and more cynical because of their work:

You're dealing with over a thousand people for eight hours a day that you just don't trust. That carries over outside of here in the way you deal with other people. My former wife used to tell me, "Since you started at the prison, you're a lot more abrupt. You're not as compassionate in the way you communicate things."

With the cynicism comes a special knowledge—a special outlook. You come to see the world inside the institution as "real" and the world outside as a "fairy-tale land." You may also have difficulty separating your on-duty and off-duty personality. A female officer indicated such a change when she said:

> You do have a tendency to "look over your shoulder," to notice more—to be more aware than before. Even when I'm not here [inside the prison], I find myself almost playing spy all the time. I find myself looking at people in a different light than I did before.

A NEW AWARENESS

You may also learn that to display much emotion is not acceptable. You learn not to appear vulnerable. One officer who had been taken hostage described how he and the others reduced the stress of the situation after being released: "I was tough. We didn't need any of this 'debriefing stuff.' We just went down to the saloon and got drunk." Again, alcohol seems to be used as a stress reducer.

You may properly feel a fear and distrust of the population you deal with. Being called to handle an unknown situation raises concern: "Your adrenalin gets pumping. You don't know whether or not something's a setup to get you into an area."

Another officer verified the reality of that danger: "I've been taken hostage and I've been stabbed and assaulted many times." In response to danger from inmates, you learn to stick together. Your colleagues become extremely important to you:

> I guess I put my life in their hands every day. I feel good about the people I work with. After you've worked with

them for a while, it's almost like you can feel what their next move is going to be and you plan yours accordingly.

As you become increasingly close to other guards at work, you may find yourself spending more and more time together off the job:

STRAINED HOME RELATIONSHIPS

We spend a lot of time together. A lot of us go bowling in the winter. Somebody put together a boat trip this summer where everybody went out on the river. After work at night you just went down to the river and BS'd and sat there.

The job becomes very important to you. You learn who you are within the institution, and it becomes more than just a job. It becomes a life: "You lived the job. In fact, we had rooms upstairs and a lot of the guys stayed here. You just lived it."

As the job and other officers become more and more important, a price is paid at home. The increased importance of work has a parallel decreased importance for the family:

I'm on my third marriage now. I've vowed that I'm going to handle this one different. I have a new start, but I'm also looking back, and it's real painful to look at my other children. I missed a lot of their growing up. I think a lot of us do that when we're spending a lot of time here. If I wasn't here at work, I was with my pals from work.

You tend not to admit problems, even to friends: "I was always there for my friends, but I never let them be there for me." Another officer described how this affected his home life: "A neighbor kid, she's five years old, said to me, 'You never smile.'"

What is it about the field of corrections that can cause such changes? As in law enforcement, a complex combination of factors are at work.

THE CORRECTIONS PROFESSION

One source of stress within the corrections profession, similar to law enforcement, is the administration. You struggle with schedules, rules and regulations, supervisors, and job responsibility. You may also feel relatively powerless and unappreciated. You may *perceive* that the administration does not support you:

> I had a supervisor that was particularly vindictive. He was coming on very hard and very strong because of personal issues, because he didn't like some of the people I knew. He used his position to try to get me demoted or suspended. Nothing ever did happen, but it was very stressful.

You are also expected to accept actions as part of your job that others would find totally unacceptable. For example, you are expected to put up with abusive language, sexual innuendos and propositions, and threats both to you and your family.

There are other stressors that "come with the job." The prisons are understaffed because hiring personnel does not seem to be a high priority item in election years. The public decries crime and the early release of criminals, but it does not seem willing to give the system the staff and support it needs to keep the criminals in jail. Often inmates have a "working relationship" with you. Yet neither of you can afford to trust the other completely, so you work in an atmosphere of tension, distrust, and the ever-present potential for danger.

This danger, however, is offset with hours of dull routine. Obviously, the prison is not in a state of riot all the time. You do not spend all your time responding to crises. Countless hours you simply wait for something to happen. While you wait, however, you cannot really relax. You cannot totally prepare for the unexpected, even though you know that at some time it *is* going to happen.

Because of this constant state of excitement inside the prison, you may find less of interest outside the institution. The adrenalin that flows during the shakedowns, confrontations with inmates, and disturbances cannot be matched elsewhere.

THE ADRENALINE RUSH

You experience the adrenalin rush and come to anticipate, often to even hope for, that rush. It can become an unconscious end in itself. As a response to stress, you may find that you expose yourself to more and more danger to get that same rush. This leaves your body in overdrive most of the time. You seldom slow down. In fact, you may stay on the premises at the prison so as not to miss any action.

THE CONSEQUENCES OF STRESS

With the "overdrive" comes the standard responses to stress, including headaches, backaches, stomach problems, high blood pressure, and heart attacks.

You are likely to find that you are alone more often, have marital problems, and seek solace in the job. This becomes a vicious cycle—as you experience more and more of these problems, you become more and more involved at work which leads to more and more of these problems.

You are not likely to stop and take personal time out. You are always "on call," and when called are definitely needed—by other people you work with, by the civilian population of the area, and by the general public to do what they are either afraid to do or choose not to. In response to these needs, you suffer. The effects of stress may accumulate until you cannot take any more.

Some officers "explode," no longer able to hold their world together. They are forced to seek help. Most correctional officers will not seek help until it is absolutely necessary. They wait until the stress buildup has created a crisis and they cannot function because of it. It is then that correctional officers find the prison bars work both ways.

"How do I spell job stress?"   HOSTAGE!

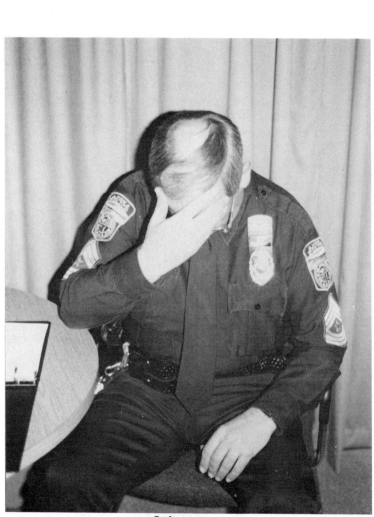

It hurts . . .

Chapter 3

A CLOSE-UP
VIEW OF STRESS

I felt like there was nowhere to go but down. Life was just too hard to live, and being dead was just so easy. And no more pain, no more internal pain. I have no idea why I didn't kill myself.

This is the ultimate reaction to stress. Stress has become a problem of increasing proportions. Business, industry, and health insurance firms are concerned about costs of employee disability as the courts award larger and larger monetary settlements for injury from work stress and allow payment for anxiety, depression, and post-traumatic stress disorder.

Stress is an elusive term which means different things to different people. Dictionary definitions of stress include: "a strain or pressure, a force exerted upon a body that tends to strain or deform its shape, to create tension, exertion." Researchers attempting to explain stress often rely on models.

MODELS OF STRESS

Among the best known models of stress are those developed by Selye, McGrath, Parr, and Violanti.

The Selye Model. Selye (1974), a pioneer in the study of stress, has described it as "the nonspecific response of the body to any demand made upon it." He further defined the concept by saying what stress was *not*. Stress is **not**:

- merely nervous tension.
- the nonspecific result of damage.
- something to be avoided.

In 1976 Selye identified certain physical responses to stress which caused changes in the body's chemical composition. He classified these responses and changes into three stages:

- The alarm reaction stage.
- The resistance stage.
- The exhaustion stage.

Alarm reaction is the initial stage of stress. During this stage you recognize some threat to safety or happiness. You become aware that your current state of affairs will not suffice to either reach your individual goals or to maintain the status quo.

During the **resistance** stage, you try to cope with the problem and your body tries to repair the damage caused during the alarm stage. You attempt to "protect yourself" both physically and mentally. These attempts continue, sometimes successfully, sometimes not.

When the attempts are successful, the situation is altered, the threat to safety or happiness is removed, and stress is removed. When these attempts are not successful, however, you may exhaust your resources. Feelings of hopelessness and a lack of control become evident. This is the **exhaustion** stage.

The McGrath Model. According to McGrath (1970), stress is more than a prescribed collection of physical responses to a particular set of circumstances. He argued that *perception* (what you believe is so) is an essential part of a comprehensive stress model. He identified four stages in stress:

- Demand on the individual.

- Perception (awareness) of that demand.
- Response to the demand.
- Consequences of response.

McGrath further explained:

> . . . stress exists not in an imbalance between objective demand and the organism's response capability, but in an imbalance between *perceived* or subjective demand and *perceived* responsecapability. One is not threatened by demands whichhe does not "receive," or by demands which heperceives himself to be capable of handling withoutundue expenditure of resources (whether or not thatjudgement is in fact correct). *One is threatened bythe anticipation that he will not be able to handleperceived demands adequately.* [Emphasis added.]

The Parr Model. Parr (1986) described psychological stress using a model consisting of four basic emotions:

- Anger.
- Anxiety.
- Depression.
- Guilt.

Anger. Parr described the anger as stemming from egocentric thinking (everything revolves around me) and from the use of "should" ("I should have been able to prevent that crime or incident").

Anxiety. The anxiety component of stress contains three major subdivisions:

- What if . . . .
- It would be awful if . . . .
- I could not stand it if . . . .

Each of the above components is future oriented and may never happen. The anxiety creates stress which, in turn, creates related issues that may never occur.

Depression. The depression component of stress manifests itself in three areas:

1. need,
2. helplessness, and
3. hopelessness.

Need. All depression begins with a perceived **need** (e.g., I need to be the best officer on the department. I need this promotion. I need new equipment).

Helplessness causes depression if you have little or no present ability to meet your *perceived* needs.

Hopelessness arises when you become convinced that your needs will *never* be met.

Guilt. Guilt has two major components: (1) a concept of wrongness and (2) self-devaluation or a belief in self-responsibility for that wrongness.

The Violanti Model. For Violanti (1982) stress is a "perceived imbalance between individual and environmental forces." He contends: "Police stress is a perceived imbalance between occupational demand and the officer's capability to effectively respond under conditions where failure *always* has important consequences." Thus, Violanti incorporates his "imbalance" concept of stress with the police or corrections occupation.

The concept of failure *always* having important consequences is an essential part in this definition. These consequences can lead to feelings of guilt, depression, and uselessness and an outlook of futility. This applies equally to correctional and police officers because "failure" for either can have serious consequences.

Other Models. Others have identified more dynamic models of stress that consider much wider definitions and include:

- Stressor characteristics.
- Characteristics of the individual.
- External variables (e.g., support systems).

Cooper (1986) has summarized these wider definitions of stress: "For some researchers it is a stimulus, for others it is an inferred inner state, and for others it is an observable response to a stimulus or a situation."

Some characteristics that must be considered when examining stress within an individual framework are age, social status, sex, preparedness, and social support. Older individuals are more likely to experience severe stress than younger individuals. Those individuals of lower social status are likely to experience a greater degree of stress than those of a higher social status. Women are believed to suffer more stress than men. When individuals are prepared for the stressful events by prior life experiences or training, such may be used to reduce some or all of the stress.

Finally, the availability of a solid support system can help alleviate or buffer the effects of stress.

A WORKING MODEL

A working model and definition of stress might consist of three components:

- The *pressure* you feel,
- from your *surroundings*,
- which forces you to *react* in some way.

You must feel some pressure or some tension, some discomfort, threat, or potential loss. The tension must originate from an external source. And you must adapt or change in some way to reduce the tension.

As noted, administrations are often *perceived* as creating stress for both police and correctional officers. You are subjected, for example, to administrative orders, rules, regulations, etc., to maintain order and enforce laws. At the same time you must obey rules for maintaining a good relationship with the populations served.

It is important to differentiate between *stressors* which are things (or events), and *stress*, which is your response. In our working model, for example, the administration may be considered as a *stressor*, i.e., perceived as stressful and thus causing *stress*, which is your response as an individual officer.

STRESSORS

Stressors can be both positive and negative. *Positive stressors* come from obtaining something wanted and pleasant. For example, the night before leaving on a vacation that has been a year in the planning is stressful. The vacation is a stressor. Certainly it is something pleasant, but it is still stressful.

Other common positive stressors include things like getting an award, purchasing a first home, having a baby, or even going on a fishing trip.

For police officers, positive stressors might include receiving a promotion or commendation, saving a child's life, or apprehending a major crime figure.

Positive stressors for correctional officers could include receiving official recognition, acknowledgement of an important service by co-workers, or a promotion.

Negative stressors originate in unpleasant situations that threaten safety or happiness. Negative stress can be prolonged and can cause inappropriate responses:

> Usually what would happen is I would get to work and take it out on some poor sap on the street that had a taillight out and a bad attitude. I would dump on him right away and feel good the rest of the night, and feel good because I'd finally satisfied justice.

COMMON NEGATIVE STRESSORS

Common negative stressors include losing someone important, losing something valuable, marital or family problems, or problems at work. Negative stressors can also include such things as administrative policies, perceived lack of administrative support, court leniency, antagonistic contacts with citizens or prisoners, physical danger (actual or perceived), and rotating work shifts.

One officer cited frustration with the police administration by saying:

> I feel that a lot of the stress coming from within the department is much greater than the stress coming from the criminals.... There seems to be a feeling nowadays that it's the administration against the police on behalf of the citizens. You expect combative situations with the criminals, but it gets real discouraging when it comes from your administration and city government, which is supposed to be working with you and supportive of you.

This same view was expressed by a correctional officer:

> People around here just want to be more respected. If the administration would reach down, give us a hand or some recognition, people would be happier, more productive. But they don't. Right now, it's an "us against them" issue.

Officers have also expressed disillusionment with their perception of the courts:

> I think the crowning blow was to see that it's almost futile to go out there and do anything about it. Ya keep putting them away, and they keep letting them out. And then new people come along, and it just doesn't stop, and it never will stop. But that's a fact of life now. I've learned that. But that's why I have a job, and it's always going to go on.

A correctional officer put it simply: "Eighty-nine out of a hundred inmates will return to the institution."

Stress is intangible, like happiness, sadness, anxiety, or fear. It can be observed and measured only through the effects it has on individuals. As you experience "stress," your specific physical and emotional responses can be measured.

THE AUTOMATIC STRESS REACTION

Once an event is perceived as stressful, your body adjusts in a number of ways. One officer described the physical effects of stress when he said: "Right now whenever there's a lot of stress my back starts to hurt." Another said:

> I think I paid a price physically. I think I've aged a lot in the time I've been a cop. There's everything from being beaten on to beating on people, to losing sleep, to rotating schedules.

In cases of extreme stress, your body prepares for the "flight or fight" syndrome. It responds to your mind's perception that something is about to happen to require the use of all your reserves. The first reaction is in the *autonomic nervous system.*

- Pupils enlarge for better vision.
- The mouth stops salivating.
- The windpipe expands.
- The breathing rate increases.
- Sweat glands are stimulated.
- Intestinal action is slowed.
- The adrenal gland is stimulated.

These physical changes are very obvious when you experience a stressful event. Your mouth gets dry, your pulse and respiration rate increase, your hands get sweaty, and you are ready for action. One officer described a situation as being:

> Twenty of the longest minutes of my life, walking back to back with shotguns, and scared this guy is going to fly around the corner and put a bullet between my eyes. We were literally walking back to back. I could feel my partner's sweat on my back, and for twenty minutes, in absolute total silence we went through that basement.

STRESS-RELATED ILLNESS

Constant exposure to stressful or potentially stressful situations can lead to stress-related illness such as emotional disorders, headaches, dental problems, stomach ulcers, and heart attacks. Prolonged exposure to stress can lead to depression and even to suicide. Officers are at risk in all these areas.

One officer said that his dentist told him stress was causing him to grind his teeth at night. His teeth were seriously wearing down. The stress was connected with his duty assignment, so he asked for a transfer. As soon as the officer was transferred, he quit grinding his teeth. Continued stress, however, led to two heart attacks.

EMOTIONAL RESPONSES TO STRESS

Emotional responses to stress can be broken into two main areas: *fear* and *anger*. The fear response is *passive*—that of *flight*. The anger response is *active*—that of *fight*. The intense emotions and related hormonal activity can affect your thinking. They can cause you to be preoccupied, cause a loss of concentration, inferior judgment, confusion, disorganization, and mental blanks.

The result of prolonged exposure to stress has frequently been referred to as "burn-out," defined by Morgenthau and Morgenthau (1980) as a syndrome including the following symptoms:

- To fail, or become exhausted by making excessive demands on energy, strength, and resources.
- A progressive process of fatigue and depletion of personal resources.
- A syndrome of physical and emotional exhaustion involving the development of negative self-concept, negative job attitudes, and loss of concern and feelings for clients.

Some common effects of this stress overload are low self-esteem, alcoholism, divorce, and suicide—certainly high prices to pay.

"You're right captain. We've got to whip these men into better shape"

REFERENCES

Cooper, R. K. (1986). *Occupational Stress in Police Work.* Doctoral Dissertation, University of Minnesota.

McGrath, J. E. As quoted in B. Koehler. (1986). *Police Stress, Post-Shooting Trauma, and Coping Efforts.* An unpublished paper, University of Minnesota.

McGrath, J. E., (Ed.) (1970). *Social and Psychological Factors in Stress.* New York: Holt, Rinehart and Winston.

Morgenthau, E.S. and J. L. Morgenthau. (1980). "Burnout—A Personal Hazard." *Journal of Correctional Education,* 31(3), 11-14.

Parr, V. E. (1986). "The Anatomy of Stress." In J. T. Reese. and H. A. Goldstein. (Eds.) *Psychological Services for Law Enforcement.* Washington, D.C.: U.S. Government Printing Office.

Selye, H. (1976). *The Stress of Life.* New York: McGraw-Hill.

Selye, H. (1974). *Stress Without Distress.* Philadelphia: J. B. Lippincott.

Violanti, J. M. "Police Stress: A Conceptual Definition." In *Police Stress.* February, 1982.

The hallway is much longer than it looks.

Chapter 4

OFFICERS AS VICTIMS

The depression and the guilt and the sense of loss, and the
sense of uselessness, and the sense of anything else that's
negative leads some people to drink, some people lose
interest in doing their job. I just lost interest in living. For
two, two and a half years I was suicidal. That's a hell of a
price to pay.

Victimization has been studied in relation to specific groups
as well as in a general, theoretical sense. The experience of
victimization renders you more vulnerable and less trusting.

You tend to become distrusting, both personally and
professionally. You cannot afford to naively trust because
such trust could be "deadly."

This professional distrust may carry into all phases of your
life. Gilmartin (1986) says: "Work in law enforcement
creates a perceptual set that ultimately causes the officer to
alter the social and sociological manner in which he or she
interacts with his or her environment." Soon you find you are
no longer as trusting as you once were of spouses, children, or
other people important in your life.

THE EFFECT OF "VICTIMIZATION"

Victimization also leaves you feeling vulnerable, no longer
omnipotent or in complete control, a totally unacceptable
situation for either a police or correctional officer. You are
always expected to have all the answers and to maintain

control of yourself and others at all times. This control is a professional requirement and becomes a personal mandate.

But "Officer Safety" training heightens your perception of vulnerability and encourages mistrust. You are made painfully aware of your potential for becoming a victim.

For most police and correctional officers the word *victim* takes on meanings very different from the rest of the world. To police officers, victim means "others." It is those you serve and implies weakness and vulnerability. These "others" need you to take care of them. They are not capable of self-care and self-protection.

To correctional officers, victim means those whom your inmates have viciously preyed upon. It is imperative to stay as far from this image as possible so as to control the inmates. For you to be seen as a victim would make your job impossible. (Guards aren't wimps.)

Police and correctional officers are, in many ways, self-precluded from becoming victims. When something happens to them that would ordinarily label someone as "victim," most officers refuse to accept that label. It may, in fact, be important that you *not* adopt the label of "victim." By not adopting the victim label:

- You can believe the terrible things you deal with daily will not happen to you.
- You can remain emotionally distant from those you serve and not experience their pain.
- You need not publicly acknowledge that you feel any emotional impact from the constant bombardment of negative experiences.
- You can better keep your family separate from your work.
- You can avoid potential conflicts in self-image (e.g., How can I take care of others when I can't take care of myself?).

IT WON'T HAPPEN TO ME

The "Just World" theory leads us to find reasons that victims become victims. For example, the burglary would not have happened had the people been more security conscious, or the man would not have been assaulted had he not walked down the street at night.

By maintaining such beliefs, even unconsciously, we protect ourselves from the psychological trauma connected with the idea of not having complete control over our lives and the ever-present possibilities of becoming a victim.

As you find reasons for other peoples' victimization, you think, "That won't happen to me because. . ." indicating you have taken precautions in your home, or you walk different places than the assault victim, or maybe even because you wear some lucky charm. This is not necessarily a logical process.

A SENSE OF FUTILITY

Police officers constantly deal with victims. You often find you cannot apprehend the victimizer, reduce the trauma of the victimization, or even tell the victim how to prevent future victimization.

Officers, most of all, realize their relative ineffectiveness in preventing the victimization of others. For example, you often cannot prevent the abused child from being returned to the victimizing parent or the abused wife from being beaten again and again before she is able to change her situation.

Correctional officers see the victimizers returning time after time, often with little or no remorse for their crimes.

NEED FOR PROTECTION

Victimization becomes extremely important to officers, and it becomes equally important that you *not* become victims yourselves. It is crucial that police officers find a way to insulate themselves from the pain of those they serve and for correctional officers to insulate themselves from the callousness of the victimizers they keep incarcerated.

. As you deal with crimes committed against vulnerable victims, it becomes increasingly difficult to maintain the belief that somehow the victim could have prevented the victimization. You must deal emotionally with the apparent senselessness of the victimization.

If a man is assaulted in a bar fight, you probably have little difficulty assigning partial blame to the victim and distancing yourself from this man's pain. If, however, a small child or an elderly woman is raped, you obviously have much more difficulty assigning even partial blame to the victim. You begin to empathize and may, thus, become a victim yourself.

You are further victimized because you realize that by sharing victims' experiences and pain you are also victimized. It becomes partially your experience and your pain.

With this realization, it becomes increasingly difficult to talk about your experiences to your spouse or others with whom you are close:

> I kept my wife and family completely separate from the department, and I never shared anything with them at all. I just didn't think they had to know what was going on out there. I mean, I'm sure I could have lived lovely without ever knowing things that I know.

If you believe that by sharing your pain you victimize others, then you must live alone with that pain.

PUBLIC EXPECTATIONS

The general public does not usually consider police or correctional officers as victims. Both are stereotyped as being tough, competent, and perhaps even cruel and uncaring. Officers are *not* generally considered victims because if they were, who would protect the public?

Since the word *victim* carries connotations of weakness and vulnerability, it is unacceptable to think of the protectors of society, maintainers of law and order, custodians of criminals, and defenders of justice as weak and vulnerable.

As police and correctional officers, you are socialized or taught in various acceptable ways to respond to victimization. The process begins with a training program before being hired and extends to post-employment training by seasoned veterans.

PRIMARY VS. SECONDARY VICTIMIZATION

To look at victimization and its relationship to police and correctional officers, it is important to differentiate between primary victims and secondary victims.

Primary victims. These are victims who are *directly* traumatized (e.g., victims of a burglary, robbery, or accident.)

Secondary victims. These are victims *indirectly* affected by the trauma. For example, the husband of a rape victim becomes a secondary victim of his wife's trauma.

OFFICERS AS PRIMARY VICTIMS

The most obvious way officers become *primary victims* is through the physical dangers associated with the job. You may be assaulted, shot at, stabbed, or even killed in the line of duty. A much more subtle, more insidious way you become a primary victim, however, is through the psychological effects of your work. This type of victimization is far less obvious, frequently contrary to established self-image, and until recently, denied to even exist by both officers and management.

In reality, a police officer who risks his/her own life to pull a child out of a burning car, only to have that child die moments later, or the correctional officer who finds an inmate he/she has helped slain by fellow inmates, is more than a secondary concerned party. They become involved victims as their initial hope is dramatically shattered within moments, replaced with feelings of deep frustration and failure.

OFFICERS AS SECONDARY VICTIMS

For the most part, however, officers seem to become *secondary victims.* You deal constantly with other people's victimization while the pain and blood are fresh and real.

In summary, you may well be victimized in the same way as ordinary citizens *and* in different ways because of your occupational role. In fact, Davis (1982) claims that: "When personally victimized, the police officer may well suffer more pervasive trauma than the citizen victim." Correctional officers are also likely to experience more traumatic effects than normal because of occupational demands.

Officers experience victimization in ways both similar and dissimilar to ordinary citizens. However, they often lack resources to effectively reduce the emotional trauma associated with such experiences.

STAGES OF VICTIMIZATION

Many authors treat victimization as a socio-psychological process, generally experienced in stages. Bard and Sangrey (1979) identified three stages: (1) Impact stage, (2) Recoil stage, and the (3) Reorganization stage

Impact stage. During the impact stage, you are likely to experience a numbing, a denial of the experience. Responses are instinctual, and initially you use older coping strategies in attempts to survive, physically and psychologically.

If you find that neither the older coping skills nor any you can mobilize during this experience have any effect, your ego defenses are shattered. You personalize the victimization, and your problem-solving abilities are radically diminished. You become unable to maintain ego integrity, losing much or all self-confidence. You may be shattered to your very core.

Recoil stage. During the recoil stage, the victimizing experience becomes central in your life. At this point you begin to pull yourself back together and work through the healing processes (physically and psychologically).

Reorganization stage. During the reorganization stage, you have adjusted to your traumatic experience and begin to reorganize your life. The victimizing experience is no longer central in your existence. The victimization has happened and has most likely changed your life (e.g., reduced trust levels).

THE VICTIMIZATION PROCESS

These three stages can be compared to the process the body undergoes, say, after a severe cut. Initially, during the *impact* phase, the wound is traumatic. You can do nothing to prevent the injury after the process has started.

Once treatment begins (e.g., an attempt to stop the bleeding), there is a shift from the impact phase to the *recoil* phase. You begin the healing process. As the cut forms a scab, it is still very tender, requiring special treatment and perhaps restricting use in that part of your body.

When the wound has healed, the pain is likely to be gone and activities are no longer restricted, as in the *reorganization* phase. A scar remains, however, a reminder of the experience and its impact on your life.

THE FOUR CAREER STAGES

Stages have also been identified within the police career and may well apply to correctional officers since the developmental progression seems very similar. Violanti (1983) has classified these four career stages:

- The alarm stage (0-5 years).
- The disenchantment stage (6-13 years).
- The personalization stage (14-20 years).
- The introspection stage (20 years and over).

According to Niederhoffer (1974), an officer's career stage tends to affect perceptions of stress, as well as the use and choice of coping mechanisms.

Note, however, that these stages are not cast in granite, but serve as guidelines to measure officers' progress through the career developmental phases.

TOWARD AN INTEGRATION OF THEORIES

In effect, Violanti's police career stages correspond with Bard and Sangrey's stages of victimization.   Figure 4-1 illustrates how the stages correspond to each other.

Stage One.   Violanti's first (alarm) stage corresponds with Bard and Sangrey's impact stage. Both stages involve similar perceptions and responses, including a numbing and feelings of being overwhelmed.

Stage Two.   Violanti's second stage corresponds with the recoil stage of victimization. During both stages, you realize the situation may well be something you cannot control.

The victimizing experience is central in your life. You feel the pain, anger, guilt, and other emotions attached to the victimizing experience.

During Bard and Sangrey's recoil stage, the victimizing experience is so much a central feature of your life that you may adopt an exclusive identity of "victim." The victim can become cynical, but almost always demonstrates reduced levels of trust in others.

Likewise, during Violanti's disenchantment stage, the occupation becomes a central feature in the your life. You are subject to experiencing overwhelming loneliness, cynicism, and hopelessness. Your occupation may become such a central feature of your life that you adopt an exclusive identity of police or correctional officer. This might be seen in the amount of time spent working, your attitude at home, and even in your choice of friends. Victims become victims 24 hours per day. By the same token, officers tend to assume their occupational identity 24 hours a day.

BARD AND SANGREY	VIOLANTI
Stage 1 - Impact	**Stage 1 - Alarm**
Victims use pre-existing skills to cope with new situations. They may become numb or disoriented. They feel vulnerable, lonely, abandoned. Problem-solving abilities radically diminish.	Officers experience real-life situations and attempt to cope with things learned through TV portrayals of police or through behavior learned in the academy. Neither coping mechanisms may be adequate. There may be confusion and uncertainty about the skills required for success.
Stage 2 - Recoil	**Stage 2 - Disenchantment**
The victimizing experience is a focal point in victims' lives. Victims must deal with anger, fear, and guilt.	Officers learn to cope with the job by adopting an attitude of distrust, suspicion. cynicism, and hopelessness. Officers perceive little hope for things to change. The department and work is a focal point in officers' lives.
State 3 - Reorganization	**Stage 3 - Personalization**
The shattered integrity of the victim is re-established. Victimization becomes less the "center of things." Unpleasant experiences related to the victimization can still affect victims' trust levels.	Goals shift from police work to personal. Less worry about the demands of "policing." Less fear of failure.
	Stage 4 - Introspection
	Least stressful time of officers' careers. May now look back on early career years without becoming emotionally involved.

Figure 4.1　An Integration of Theories

Stages Three and Four. Bard and Sangrey's reorganization stage of victimization corresponds to Violanti's third (personalization) and fourth (introspection) stages. In the reorganization stage, you have begun to reorganize your world, and the victimizing experience is no longer central. At this stage, you shift priorities. The victimizing experience becomes less important, while other factors assume higher priority.

Likewise, during the personalization and introspection stages of the police and correctional careers, you begin to shift priorities from the job to other interests and activities. You come to realize that you can be a productive member of the community—you are more than just a police or correctional officer.

Movement through the Stages. Although officers generally proceed through all stages, they progress at different speeds. You may progress through the stages so fast, it may appear you skipped a stage. Or you may get stuck in a stage and stay there for years.

A number of variables affect your progress, including age, sex, previous experience, and the socialization process within the department or prison.

It becomes problematic if you get stuck in either the first or second developmental stage. If you are stuck in the first developmental stage, you may spend almost all your time trying to get into the police or correction world. This precludes involvement with your occupational world and places you in a position where you are constantly subjected to secondary victimization with no time to recover.

In addition, in this stage you are not yet accepted as a member of the group. You are most likely to be denied whatever solace is available from other officers. As you become isolated from the world that is *not* "police" or "corrections," you are still not completely accepted into the world that *is* "police" or "corrections."

If you are stuck in the second stage, you may see the world as a terrible place with few bright spots. You may experience little happiness, joy, or satisfaction in the world you see now, and have little if any hope for a better world in the future.

The isolation is further strengthened by an inability to display any weakness or vulnerability. Since you have connected weakness and vulnerability with those you serve, your isolation is believed to be another way of preventing your own victimization.

Ironically, the very isolation you believe protects you often takes its own toll. The isolation itself victimizes:

> I'm not close to people, friendship-wise. There's only maybe a couple of people that I would consider close friends. I don't want other people to be close friends or to get close to me, and they haven't. I don't want them to know my weak points or my Achilles heel. So it's easier for me to be known as an asshole than to have to be one.

FIVE POSSIBILITIES OF BECOMING A VICTIM

Mendelsohn (1976) says people in general may be victims of:

- Crime.
- Self (e.g., suicide).
- Anti-social behavior (individual or collective).
- Technology.
- Uncontrolled forces of nature and the environment.

Police and correctional officers are also at risk to all five ways of becoming victims.

Crime. Police officers obviously have an intimate relationship with crime, not always as primary victims, yet frequently as secondary victims. It is a unique relationship in that you are usually a third party, neither perpetrator nor victim, yet interacting closely with both.

In describing that "unique" relationship, Krupnick and Horowitz (1980) state that while the officer has had no part in the victimizing experience, the rage of the crime victims may be displaced onto the police officers responding to the call. This seems likely to happen because the officers are handy, bound by social and occupational constraints, and it is usually safe to vent anger towards the officer.

Correctional officers do not live in the world of victims, but they are constantly reminded that victims exist by their relationship with the inmates.

Self. Second, that officers frequently become victims of "self" can be inferred using their high rates of:

- alcoholism.
- divorce.
- suicide.
- indirect self-destructive behavior.

Anti-Social Behavior. Police and correctional officers are likely to become victims of anti-social behavior, either individually or collectively.

Personally, you may become a victim of anti-social behavior when you are stereotyped into anonymity, relegated to the role of "police officer" or "prison guard" in any location or social setting.

Professionally you may become a victim when you are thrust into the role of maintaining social order, for example, monitoring a demonstration where no crime has been committed, maintaining order at a strike scene, or intervening in a domestic dispute where no crime has occurred.

Correctional officers frequently deal with anti-social individuals and groups of inmates. You are constantly on the alert for such behavior in the form of crime or riots within the prison itself.

Technology. Police officers become victims of technology in several ways. Poorly serviced equipment is one way you find yourself as a victim. A poorly maintained squad car or a radar unit not recently or accurately calibrated are examples. In addition, criminals seem to have access to more advanced computer technology and weaponry, frequently making you a victim of such technology. Consequently, you must maintain a working knowledge of such equipment for safety reasons, to

prevent "crimes of technology," and to apprehend "technological criminals."

Correctional officers also experience technological problems. Many prisons are extremely outdated. They are also
overcrowded, understaffed, and the equipment is often of the
technology from ten to fifteen years ago. While new technol-
ogies would greatly aid you in your work, it is generally not
cost-effective to install such equipment in existing prisons.
And prisons don't seem to wear out.

Uncontrolled Forces of Nature. The critical role of the police
during natural disasters was demonstrated in 1989 on the east
coast in Charleston when Hurricane Hugo's 50-mile-per-hour
winds hit, leaving the city's center under three feet of water.
It was again graphically demonstrated on the west coast when
an earthquake measuring 7.1 on the Richter scale hit the San
Francisco bay area during the rush hour causing fires, power
outages, and widespread massive destruction. In both instances police were faced not only with medical emergencies but
also with widespread looting.

While serving during or right after a natural disaster, you
may become both a primary victim (of the disaster) and a
secondary victim (through dealing with the primary victimization of others).

In fact, during such disasters, frequently other secondary
victims (relatives of people killed in the disaster) become of
utmost concern. Again, as you work with these secondary
victims, you must re-examine your own role and monitor the
effects of the disaster on yourself.

Should a natural disaster strike a prison, the consequences
could be terrible. Not only would correctional officers be
forced to deal with injury and death, but they would also be
required to try to maintain control of the inmates.

In summary, police and correctional officers both face a
possibility for victimization because of the nature of their
work. You can become a victim in the same way as ordinary
citizens, *and* you experience an increased risk of "victimization" because of your occupational choice.

KEY COMPONENTS OF VICTIMIZATION

Two key components of victimization are: (1) suffering and
(2) blamelessness. Several different aspects of those components contribute to officers' status as victims. Suffering occurs
in three areas: physical, emotional, and social.

Physical suffering is readily identified by many officers:
"There is certainly a physical price that I've paid. I've had my
teeth operated on three times; a gum disease, basically stress
from grinding my teeth."   Another officer said: "The most
evident [price] for me is that I have had two heart attacks."

Emotional suffering is described by an officer who said: "I
think the main price anyone pays has to do with their mental
attitude."

This price is often displayed as inappropriate and restricted
affect: "We're still into the old 'John Wayne syndrome'
type thing, be strong and smile; but *don't ever cry*. Be strong
and silent, suffer in silence, and if that's your lot in life, just
put up with it."

Another officer said: "The only emotion that I can show
effectively as a cop is anger. I live on anger, and I live on
jokes."

Many male officers have expressed a desire to feel tenderness when appropriate, but state they are unable to do so:
"I've become pretty numb to feelings. Personal emotions, like
affection or love, are pretty well pounded down."

On the other hand, some male officers have expressed an
inability to control their emotions: "Well, I cry a lot. That's
not a real manly, macho, policeman thing to do, but I've kind
of given up trying to fight it, because it's kind of the only
outlet I have."

Social suffering and its consequences have also been identified by officers. Your range of social contacts may be severely
limited by your status as an officer. As one officer said:
"You find your group of friendship and your socialization

getting smaller and smaller, and then you wind up with police people."

You may feel isolated from the community in part from your perception of your social status: "There seems to be a feeling by some people that public servants are second-class citizens."

This sentiment is expanded by another officer: "Basically it's our job to uphold the law, yet often we are not afforded the opportunity to receive the same protection from the same law that we provide to other people."

Personality changes were identified by an officer who said: "I don't know how it's possible to have the kind of negative attitude which is totally necessary for doing this job and still remain an 'up' person."

Blamelessness. The other component of victimization is blamelessness. Officers are blameless in several ways. You may be initially naive, not knowing what you were getting into when you became a police or correctional officer. You probably expected to be liked, admired, and trusted by the public. You probably expected to be appreciated when you did your job well. You also may have soon discovered, however, that while the public wants laws enforced, no one wants the laws enforced when it applies to them personally.

Everyone knows that drunk drivers kill, yet drunk drivers are frequently extremely incensed when they are arrested because *they know* that they would not have killed anyone. Few drivers say, "Thank you, officer," when given a speeding ticket.

Correctional officers learn that while the public wants criminals kept locked up, few want to be the one who does that job. The public wants the criminals tucked quietly away, "out of sight—out of mind."

Another part of blamelessness is an expressed lack of control. You may have changed since beginning your career, and have little or no control over the direction or extent of the change: "I know one thing, I'd become something totally different than what I was brought up to be by my mom and dad, no two ways about it." One officer described these changes in general by saying: "Most of the people that come into this type of work are real high quality human beings, not necessarily highly educated or anything like that, but just good human beings. And then they get messed up."

MOVING PAST BLAMELESSNESS AND VICTIMIZATION

While you may be initially "innocent," such innocence is soon lost. To continue describing yourself as "blameless" is no longer appropriate. As you progress through the developmental stages, you continue to be an officer and continue to subject yourself to such experiences for different reasons.

You may stay because you are married, have children, and need the financial security the occupation provides. You may stay because you are afraid to try something new or because you have found acceptance within the occupational group. Or you may stay because you have only a few years left to collect a pension:

> I'm here mainly for the benefits, and after you've got that much time in, what else can you do? You got a guy that's been here ten years and he's in his thirties, there's not much else he can do.

Even when you progress into the reorganization stage, you are likely to still be scarred by your occupation. You should, however, adjust and find new meaning in your work. Police and corrections *can* become personally rewarding careers.

DEPARTMENTAL RESPONSE

Reiser and Geiger (1984) note that police and other law enforcement agencies have had difficulty addressing the problems of officers who have become victims of stress.

Police agencies are frequently perceived as bureaucratic, unsympathetic, and a renewed source of stress for officers (Cooper, 1986). The administrations of these agencies must understand that many officers *are* secondary victims and provide resources for those under stress. This would do much to lessen the impact of such victimization on officers' lives.

Many correctional officers find themselves in much the same role—perceiving their department as bureaucratic, unsympathetic, and a source of stress: "Why can't they be helpful and supportive instead of all this petty bullshit?"

Instead of finding emotional support and stress reduction, however, you may be re-victimized by the department through inappropriate, unnecessary, and unwanted job assignments or transfers, excessive forms and paperwork, and misunderstood, unwarranted, and cumbersome procedures. (See Chapter 18).

"What a night."

REFERENCES

Bard, M., and D. Sangrey. (1979). *The Crime Victim's Book.* New York: Basic Books.

Cooper, R. K. (1986). *Occupational Stress in Police Work.* Doctoral Dissertation, University of Minnesota.

Davis, B. (1982). "Burnout." *Police Magazine.* 5(3), pp. 9-18.

Gilmartin, K. M. (1986). "Hypervigilance: A Learned Perceptual Set and Its Consequences on Police Stress." In J. T. Reese and H.A. Goldstein, *Psychological Services for Law Enforcement.* Washington, D.C.: U.S. Government Printing Office, pp.445-452.

Krupnick, J.L. and M. J. Horowitz. (1980). "Victims of Violence: Psychological Responses, Treatment Implications." [Special Issue], *Evaluation and Change.* 42-46.

Mendelsohn, B. (1976). "Victimology and Contemporary Society's Trends." In E.C. Viano, (Ed.) *Victims and Society,* (pp. 7-28). Washington, D.C.: Visage Press.

Neiderhoffer, A., (1974). *Behind the Shield.* New York: Doubleday.

Reiser, M. and S. P. Geiger. (1984). "Police Officer as Victim." *Professional Psychology: Research and Practice,* 15(3), pp. 315-323.

Violanti, J.M. (1983). "Stress Patterns in Police Work: A Longitudinal Study." *Journal of Police Science and Administration.* 11(2), pp. 211-216.

These officers almost lost their lives—you don't expect to drown driving down a city street!

Chapter 5

POST-TRAUMATIC
STRESS DISORDER

This is combat! I mean that's like saying that a guy can
spend 20 years as a soldier. I mean it's one thing to be a
peace-time soldier, but I mean to be in the trenches fighting
and killing, and I'm not saying we kill a lot, but I mean we
see a lot of shit and we also deal with a lot of shit. This is
combat. This *is* combat. That may sound hokey, but the
reality is, it's a combat. It's just a different kind of combat.

Police officers suffering emotional problems have been
compared to Vietnam veterans with post-traumatic stress
disorder (PTSD). You may see yourself as involved in a form
of war with little popular support. Correctional officers also
may see themselves as being on the edge. The prison could
erupt into a battlefield at any moment. With inmates greatly
outnumbering guards, the prospect of an all-out riot is
frightening:

I've been involved in some major things here. We had a riot
that I was involved in. I was surrounded by literally dozens
of inmates at one time where it was a very life-threatening
situation. They were indicating that we weren't going to
make it out of there.

In describing the Vietnam war, Parson (1984) indicated
that the lack of front lines and never knowing who the enemy
was intensified the post-traumatic stress disorder. And just as

55

police officers are not concerned about stopping all crime, Vietnam soldiers were not concerned about "winning" the war. Parsons (p. 10) said:

> Everyone is suspect and poses a potential threat to one's life and safety. No one can be trusted, and there are no front lines to demarcate areas of danger from those of relative safety. The soldier in Vietnam was not as concerned about winning the war as he was about surviving–staying alive by constantly watching. He watched everything that moved and he watched the inanimate–not knowing who the enemy would be, when he would strike, or from where.

Likewise, police and correctional officers are trained to be constantly alert. The unknown enemy is a stressor. You could just as easily be killed by an elderly little lady or a trustee as by a young thug.

In describing lack of popular support, one officer said: "We are the front line when the citizens want somebody to bitch at because they don't like what's happening in this town or any town in the country. We're the most convenient. We're the scapegoats." Similar conditions have been called "survivor syndrome" (Kijak and Funtowicz, 1982) and "rape trauma syndrome" (Burgess and Holstrom, 1974).

When the public needs a scapegoat for something that goes wrong in a prison, a riot, hostage situation, or killing, they seldom blame the administration. Instead they tell the correctional officers that they "didn't follow procedure" or that they "got careless."

Post-traumatic stress disorder is not new. Sir Walter Scott (1908) wrote of this malady:

> *Soldier rest! thy warfare o'er*
> *Dream of fighting fields no more:*
> *Sleep the sleep that knows not breaking,*
> *Morn of toil, nor night of waking.*
> –Lady of the Lake

PTSD, according to the American Psychiatric Association (1980), refers to: "the development of characteristic symptoms following a psychologically traumatic event that is generally outside the range of human experience."

POST-TRAUMATIC STRESS DISORDER CRITERIA

The American Psychiatric Association (1985) presents the following diagnostic criteria for post-traumatic stress disorder:

I. Existence of a recognizable stressor that would evoke significant symptoms of distress in almost anyone.

II. Re-experiencing of the trauma as evidenced by at least one of the following:

   A. recurrent and intrusive recollection of the event
   B. recurrent dreams of the event
   C. sudden acting or feeling as if the traumatic event were reoccurring, because of an association with an environmental or ideational (mental) stimulus

III. Numbing of responsiveness to or reduced involvement with the external world, beginning some time after the trauma, as shown by at least one of the following:

   A. markedly diminished interest in one or more significant activities
   B. feeling of detachment or estrangement from others
   C. constricted affect

IV. At least two of the following symptoms that were not present before the trauma:

   A. hyper-alertness or exaggerated startle response
   B. sleep disturbance
   C. guilt about surviving when others have not, or about behavior required for survival
   D. memory impairment or trouble concentrating
   E. avoidance of activities that arouse recollection of the traumatic event
   F. intensification of symptoms by exposure to events that symbolize or resemble the traumatic event

Police officers involved in shooting incidents often fit this diagnostic criteria. For example, Cohen (1980) says that of the more than 100 United States police officers who kill someone in the line of duty each year, almost all will suffer reactions that include nightmares, flashbacks, and severe depression. He says such officers tend to withdraw and to experience marital difficulties.

For a correctional officer the experience of being held hostage may well evoke a traumatic incident response. In such a case, you are held powerless by inmates who may have little or no respect for human life and to whom you are only a tool—to be used and, if necessary, used up.

It is not only officers involved in shooting incidents or hostage situations who may fit the diagnostic criteria. The nature of police and corrections work puts officers at risk of post-traumatic stress disorder because of the acute trauma attached to many of the calls for service or assistance.

PTSD AND THE POLICE-CORRECTIONS EXPERIENCE

Police officers, indeed, are frequently exposed to traumatic events "generally outside the range of human experience":

> I think it certainly expands one's view of reality. You end up getting in situations that you would never see unless you were a policeman, or unless you were a victim or a suspect. You see the whole spectrum as a policeman.

Correctional officers also frequently see criminals and crime in a unique way. You see criminals as individuals, yet are also well aware of the serious crimes they've committed.

Another officer differentiated the police experience from that of the civilian population when he said:

> Citizens know that there's good guys and bad guys, and they know that a certain percentage of people commit crimes. But I don't think they fully understand it. It's like me going to my next door neighbor and telling him that I got into a

chase where it lasts five minutes and I'm going ninety miles per hour, and he says, "Oh, gee, that's really great." But they really have no in-depth comprehension of what I'm talking about.

Or if I go to a DOA where I say the guy's been there for two weeks, where we've picked him up and his ass sticks to the floor. He's going, "Oh, wow, really?" They're agreeing with what I'm telling them, but without really being there, they have no idea what the hell I'm talking about.

Police officers also distinguish their experience from that of other "helping professionals":

It's like the people at General Hospital. The doctors and nurses, they can relate, but they can't relate to the whole job. They can only relate to their part of it. They see physical pain and physical dismemberment and that type of thing. The psychologist is going to see people psychologically crippled by things that have happened to them. The coroners will see death. They all see their piece of it, but they don't see it all, and sometimes all in one night.

One officer described his response to his first homicide call like this:

When I first came on the job, that first homicide I went to was where two guys shot it out in the street and they both ended up killing each other. That bothered me--seeing the blood and seeing the holes and seeing these teenagers--two dead teenagers.

You frequently are involved in a *secondary* way in traumatic situations such as robbery, sexual assault, burglary, and even homicide because you are not only dispatched to such scenes, but expected to function "normally." Certainly all are traumatic situations. You are probably involved in a *primary* way with less frequency. But such situations are at least of equal, if not much more, importance. Police officers see this on the "outside" while correctional officers deal with the same things "inside.""

Use of Deadly Force. No matter how justified, the use of deadly force is always traumatic.   Ten years after being involved in a shooting, one police officer reported: "I shot and killed this kid that had robbed a place, and I thought that he or his partner shot at me. As it turned out they had not. They were armed, but they had not shot at me. But I thought they had. That was traumatic."

These experiences take a toll on police officers. There is pain and change and life goes on:

> When I get off I would just like to forget about it, but I can't. Sometimes you go home at night and some of the things you've seen during the daytime, you think about them at night and you dream about them. I guess I just think about it to myself until I can't think about it any more and go on, just go on.

Intentional taking of life for a correctional officer is a more remote possibility. Yet if you are stationed in a tower, the issue is of concern. You may have to shoot an escaping inmate. While the action is completely justified, you may still question your act, face an adversarial press, and be subjected to a deluge of bureaucratic red tape.

SHATTERING OF ASSUMPTIONS

Janoff-Bulman (1985) has proposed that post-traumatic stress following victimization experiences is largely due to a shattering of basic assumptions the victims held about themselves and their world. This includes a belief in:

- Personal invulnerability.
- The world as meaningful.
- The self as positive.

Personal vulnerability. Officers' belief in *personal invulnerability* is challenged daily. Each day brings reminders of officers injured or killed. At roll call or just during coffee breaks, you may talk of a violent traffic arrest made by another officer and that officer's subsequent trip to the hospital—or the morgue. Correctional officers may talk of problems in a particular cell block or of an officer assaulted by inmates.

The statistical summaries are monthly reminders of how many officers nationally are injured or killed.

The world as meaningful. Further, *the world* is not perceived *as meaningful.* Meaning requires some sense of fairness and order. You may lose your sense of fair-play quickly:

> When I started I used to have a sense that when you arrest these guys they went to jail, there was a sense of justice and fair play, and now I don't have that sense. I mean, I do my job because I'm getting paid to do it. I'll make the arrest, but I don't have any feeling that anything's ever going to happen that's going to make a whole lot of differences to this guy. I don't think he's [the criminal] going to pay a debt to society. I don't think he paid his debt to the victim. I think the victim gets screwed over. It's really depressing to think that there's no justice, that there's not a sense of fair play.

The world is not orderly, and you are forced to deal not only with the effects of violence, but its randomness as well.

The self as positive. Perception of *self as positive* is also often difficult when you have just been involved in a traumatic experience. It is difficult to see anything as positive after looking at a dead child, or even worse, after taking a child's life. Or, after seeing the same people returning to prison again and again, you may feel a sense of futility and question why these criminals are ever released at all. This lack of positive feelings leads to a sense of powerlessness:

> It's my firm opinion that if the public didn't know it, the police department could stay home and nothing would change. The crime rate would stay the same. Nothing would change. There might be some problems with a medical emergency, but basically it would stay the same.

Singleton and Teahan (1978) have stated that in addition to any physical injury a police officer may suffer, the more severe injury is often to the individual's ego:

> I really thought I was an important son-of-a-gun, what I did was making a difference, and who I was, was important. After having had a heart attack and re-evaluating everything, I lost a lot of my ego. I lost a lot of my self-importance.

You probably became a police officer to "help people," and are disillusioned when you find you cannot:

> You can do little things on the side to make people feel better, and once in a while you get a case you can really work up and really get something good out of it. But, for the most part, as I found out the hard way, cops aren't the ones that are going to fix the system. It has gotta be somebody else.

POWERLESSNESS VS. CONTROL

Reiser and Geiger (1984) went beyond this step when they said: "Trauma appears to result from the puncturing of the officer's prior illusion of control and invulnerability. Inherent in the authority role is the assumption of being in absolute charge of one's environment":

> It's real hard for me to give up control. I had a relationship that ended over basically the control issue. I have to control the situations right from the get go. If you don't take control, I think you've lost it. It's just something that I've learned to do, and that definitely has carried over into my personal life.

Another described the need to be in charge this way:

> For me one of the worst feelings is not being in control, not being able to handle it. Control is a big issue. I feel real panicky if I don't have control of something, or at least have a system of gaining control. I like to know what is going to happen. I do that by trying to have total control at all times.

THE SURVIVOR'S SYNDROME

Krystal and Niederland (1968) have identified a "survivor's syndrome," the manifestations of which include:

- Depression.
- Inability to handle anger.
- Anxiety.
- Paranoia.
- Sleep disturbances with recurrent nightmares.

Depression. The manifestation of depression was described by one officer who said:

> I work in a low-income district that is real violent and alcoholic. And seeing that for eight hours a day, it is real hard for me to remember that there are real bright people who study and grow and are happy. I just see these people with their horrible pathetic lives. I know there is a real tendency towards depression.

Inability to Handle Anger. Not only is depression a common problem, you may also find yourself unable to handle anger:

> I was extremely irritable. My wife noticed that things would irritate me a lot quicker. I didn't have the patience I used to have, and I was losing my temper with her quite a bit.

Anxiety. The third manifestation of the survivor's syndrome, intense anxiety, can be triggered by situational reminders of the traumatic event:

> When I'm in a situation where I'm involved in a "shots fired" call or even when I hear another squad going on a "shots fired," I start to think about it [the shooting this officer was involved in]. In other words, my heart starts to beat harder, and I start to get wound up about it.
> When I went back there on calls. When I went in there [where the shooting occurred] my wounds would start to

hurt, even though they shouldn't. And when I walked out, they would quit hurting.

For correctional officers such situational reminders take the form of putting on the uniform to return to work after a traumatic incident or walking through the cell block where the incident occurred. Even the time of shift or activities during the shift can bring back memories of a traumatic event.

Paranoia. You may well find yourself becoming more suspicious after becoming a police or correctional officer. One officer saw herself as more than just suspicious as a result of police work: "It just affected everything—my attitude with my family, on the job—instead of making me less stressed, I became more stressed because I was getting paranoid."

A female officer described the following actions after she was involved in a shooting:

> I was worried his friends and relatives would try to do me harm. A carload of assholes went by my parents' house, they're listed in the [telephone] book, and made threatening gestures out of the car. I was very careful right after that occurred.
>
> I was very secretive for a time about who I was and where I lived because my name was in the paper that I had done this. Since then I wouldn't write my name on an envelope for return. I would just write my initials.
>
> I gave my work address for more than a year after it happened. I gave it all the time. I wouldn't give my address. If a store wanted an address, I would give a work address or some other address.
>
> Even when I went to apply for a part-time job a short time after the shooting, I didn't want the employer to know where I lived which seems pretty paranoid.

A correctional officer stated that after being lied to so often: "It was hard to trust anybody."

Sleep Disturbances with Recurrent Nightmares. Common nightmares for police officers involve time distortion and feelings of powerlessness. Frequently officers involved in shootings have recurrent nightmares. You may dream about a bullet leaving your gun in slow motion and falling ineffectively to the ground or about shooting a person repeatedly without effect:

> In some of the dreams I had been shot, people were holding me and stabbing me. I was being chased by crowds of people. I am being held and then shot by other parties. It is always a group. It is never one person just chasing me.
>
> In some of the dreams I shoot back, and the crowd keeps coming at me. It's like nothing is happening. And they just come up to me and grab me and stab me. The bullets don't seem to stop them. They just keep coming.

Police shootings are not the only traumatic events that can cause nightmares, however. One officer reported that she had consistent nightmares after witnessing a teenage boy shoot himself in the head. Over and over she kept seeing the boy's face and watching helplessly as the boy shot himself.

For correctional officers such nightmares can easily revolve around traumatic events within the prison. You may experience powerlessness again and again when you are unable to prevent a suicide or a homicide, or an assault on yourself or other officers.

SITUATIONAL REMINDERS

Police and correctional officers are frequently exposed to situational reminders of the traumatic events they experienced. These reminders include simply preparing for the job, geographic clues, calls of a similar nature, the responses of other officers, as well as newspaper articles and court hearings.

Preparing For the Job. Getting ready to go on duty can remind you of a traumatic event. Simply getting into the squad car or strapping on a gunbelt after a traumatic event can be a reminder of that event. The gunbelt, for example, reminds officers involved in shootings that they must be prepared to take yet another life if necessary, experience the same confusion and trauma as last time, and go through the nightmare again. As one officer involved in a shooting incident said:

> I thought when I put the gunbelt on that realistically, the chances were that I wouldn't have to use it again. Had I thought I would have to use it again, I don't know if I could have gone back to work. I was looking at statistically what the chances were, and I guess I spent a lot of time thinking about that before I went back. I was hyper-alert. I kept telling myself, "If it happens again, I'm going to be ready."

Putting on a gunbelt can also remind you of your own mortality. After a close brush with death, you feel you have an understanding that people who have not faced death do not have:

> I still get up and take a shower and get ready to go to work and still see the scar on my chest. And it still makes me wonder, "Is today going to be the day?" It's hard to really plan your life, to realize that tomorrow you may not be here. Everybody's aware that they could die, but when you're really confronted with it and you come that close to dying, you think, "Boy! I could be gone so quick!"

As the prison door slams behind correctional officers, they may realize that they are back "inside" and must again prepare to deal with trauma.

Geographic and Similar Calls Reminders. You may be constantly bombarded by geographic reminders of traumatic events. Each time you drive through a specific intersection, memories may resurface of the boy and girl killed there in a motorcycle accident. Or each time you drive past a specific address, you may be reminded of a suicide you responded to there.

Each time a correctional officer walks through a particular cell block, it may bring back memories of an assault or a suicide.

Calls of a similar nature can also remind you of past traumatic events in several different ways. Every call for "shots fired" does not result in a homicide. Many such calls, in fact, are simply neighbors who cannot distinguish between gunshots and firecrackers. Yet, if you respond to a call for "shots fired" and find a gory homicide scene, you make a connection that does not easily disappear. Each time you are dispatched to a call for "shots fired," you are likely to re-experience the traumatic event:

> I remember that first night [back] on the street. I got a call on "shots fired," and you know that got the heart beating hard and I thought, "Oh, here we go again, the same routine. He's going to have a gun on him." I get real worked up.

When correctional officers respond to a call of an unruly crowd in a cell block, memories of trauma are likely to resurface.

Responses of Other Officers. The greetings of other officers may also be a reminder of a traumatic event. You may have never spoken to some officers before, but if you are involved in a shooting, for example, everyone knows who you are—by name:

> At first it's a real attention getter. I mean I've got people on the police department that know my first name, my last name, know where I'm working, know a lot about me. I don't know anything about them. I don't even know their names. You become well known overnight.

News Stories and Court Battles. As you experience traumatic events, for example, a shooting in which you are forced to take a life, the traumatic event does not simply end. Even after the reports are written and you go home, there is so much more—the newspaper articles, the responses from other officers, and the court battles that generally follow, with you as a defendant in a civil suit.

You tend to generalize those stimuli that remind you of a traumatic event. Each time you think about the newspaper articles or even read about other officers in the paper, you are reminded of your own personal trauma. You *know* you cannot tell "your side" to the press, but those on the other side can and *do*.

Court battles also continue the trauma for you. Each time you are brought to court you are forced to relive the traumatic event as well as to justify your actions in that particular situation. This is, of course, done in an adversarial setting with attorneys challenging your motivation, training, and actions and only allowing half statements. A typical exchange might go like this:

Defense Attorney: "Did you go there?"

Officer: "Yes, but I didn't go in."

Defense Attorney: "Just answer my question. Did you *go* there?"

Officer: "Yes, but . . ."

Defense Attorney: "That will be all, officer."

It is important to know you did right. Courtroom battles continue to challenge your belief in your own competence:

> I was really just concerned as far as inside I knew I had done the right thing. But I was waiting for somebody to tell me that everything's going to be all right, especially after I had heard that the person had died. I wanted to make sure that I still remained the good guy and everybody thought I had done the right thing. I wanted everybody to understand exactly what had taken place.

REPEATED EXPOSURE TO TRAUMATIC EVENTS

In addition to frequent reminders of past traumatic experiences, repeated exposure to other traumatic events makes recovery difficult. Police and correctional officers are routinely exposed to trauma while on duty. In fact, it is common to be exposed to several traumatic events within the same shift. And the potential for a traumatic event is *always* present.

As you experience traumatic events, you must function within that event, setting personal feelings aside. Often, before you have a chance to emotionally process the effects of one traumatic event, you are exposed to a second and perhaps even a third such event. As the impact of these events accumulate, it becomes increasingly difficult to deal with any of it:

> You saw something that really bothered you. But you wouldn't admit it. You'd make some joke about it or something. You'd come out sideways rather than coming straight out. So you'd still carry it around with you for a while until you forgot about it or something more horrifying replaced it. And then you'd worry about that.

You constantly deal with others who have experienced or are experiencing a traumatic event. This contagious effect interferes with the healing process. It can be an emotional treadmill:

> The feelings of these people–the victims and suspects that you deal with–the victims or the suspects, when you see them, are always so intense. If they've been burglarized, they're upset because their "castle's" been burglarized. Or the suspect's mad because you've caught him. And your feelings are always going at a fever pitch.

PTSD — THE BIG PICTURE

Specific characteristics and manifestations of post-traumatic stress disorder often occur because you cannot respond to traumatic situations as most people can. The "normal" initial response to a traumatic event is usually numbness. Most people shut down their input systems and allow the "self" time to process what has happened.

Police and correctional officers, however, often have neither the time nor the luxury of this normal response. You are often required to intervene to prevent further injuries, to help victims with physical injuries, to help others who have become non-functional because of the trauma, or to end continuing trauma by intervening in this situation with an arrest or additional violence.

When correctional officers intervene in a fight between two inmates, there is always a concern that the fight is a ruse to entrap you or that the inmates watching will join the fight and attack you.

Or consider a domestic call where you must physically subdue one spouse and then have both spouses shift their violence from each other and attack you.

Many situations are physically dangerous. For example, if you respond to a homicide scene, you certainly need to pay attention to the perpetrator so as not to become the next victim. Even while directing traffic at a fatal freeway accident you need to pay attention so as not to be run over by another car whose driver is drunk or not paying attention.

Rather than being able to actually distance yourself from a traumatic event, you are frequently required to set the affective components of that event aside to deal with later. Later can be a time you never get to by choice. But later *will* force the event back into consciousness.

THE TWO-PHASE MODEL

The two most common phases of post-traumatic stress disorder are *denial* and *intrusion*. Following a traumatic event, officers subjected to PTSD will experience either a denial of the event or the event will become an intrusive presence in their daily lives.

An apparently healthy adaptation and a quick return to normalcy with little or no obvious effect from a traumatic event is often, in reality, *denial*. Such denial is a normal response for police and correctional officers. You are under extreme pressure to continue functioning during and immediately after exposure to trauma. Often a life is at stake, either your own, that of someone else, or both.

You are trained to respond to traumatic situations impersonally, objectively. You are taught to *not* process the events on an emotional level until much later, if at all. You are trained to respond automatically, to "be professional."

Denial. Denial usually takes one of three tracks:

- Denial of the trauma itself.
- Denial of any personal involvement.
- Denial of the effect.

You may deny any trauma attached to an incident. It is just "business as usual": "It isn't great to take someone's life. If you have to, fine. It won't bother me if I have to. If it happens again, I'd do it again."

Denial of personal involvement is shown by officers who say: "There was nothing I could have done. He made his own decision to kill himself." To say "he made his own decision" is a way to wash your hands of the matter, implying you were not involved in the crucial part of the traumatic event; in this case, the decision to commit suicide.

Denial of the effect as the direct result of the trauma is part of a need to maintain control. You may feel that to be affected by traumatic events symbolizes weakness and may indicate an inability to handle the job. Therefore, you deny any "feelings" surrounding the traumatic experience.

Intrusion. During the *intrusive* phase of post-traumatic stress disorder, you begin to experience problems. You begin to re-experience the event through intrusive thoughts, memories, or visions:

> The dreams didn't come at first. At first I was convinced this was a legitimate shooting. After all, he brought it upon himself. I had absolutely no choice in the matter, and I'm not going to have any problems with this. And I maintained that for a couple of months until, out of the blue, I started

getting these strange dreams. And that brought on other problems.

HOW INDIVIDUAL VARIABLES INFLUENCE TRAUMA

While many officers experience PTSD, research indicates that the majority of symptoms (e.g., nightmares, intrusive flashbacks, etc.), are experienced primarily by officers involved in fatal traumatic incidents. Other post-traumatic stress symptoms (e.g., emotional distancing, hyper-alertness, cynicism) are experienced by larger numbers of officers.

Because response to traumatic situations varies among individual officers, just which symptoms will be exhibited depends on a number of variables:

- Pre-trauma personality.
- Pre-trauma stress.
- Type of trauma.
- Interpretation of the traumatic event.
- Reaction.
- Mediating variables.
- Post-trauma stress.

Pre-trauma Personality. Of primary importance is whether you perceive you have an internal or an external locus of control. Trauma seems easier to accept when it is an "act of God" rather than something that "could have been prevented." Often external control is emphasized to protect officers from the brunt of the trauma.

Internal Locus. Trauma is exaggerated when you have an *internal locus of control* and assume you are to blame for the situation. Given a need for control, it is often difficult to "let go" of a perception of control, even though such a perception is illusionary:

> I don't think I would have done anything different based on the information that was given, but you still wonder. You wonder if he wouldn't still be alive today if I had done things

differently. For a long time that's why I kept playing the scenario over and over again, trying to convince myself that what I did was right, even though I knew I was right.

If you examine situations with an internal locus of control, you look for what you may have done "wrong" so you can make adjustments and prevent the situation from reoccurring.

External Locus. An *external locus of control* makes the situation less personal. You realize there may well have been no way to avoid the situation: "Realistically, there's nothing that can prevent something like this from happening. There's nothing you can do about it. Live with it . . . ."

Pre-trauma Stress affects your responses because you can respond to only so much stress. Each person has a limit. If you are close to that limit when another traumatic event occurs, you are more likely to go over the edge. Additional stress may be too much for you. You may be unable to process the current trauma.

One officer who had recently been involved in several traumatic experiences examined his store of coping resources and sadly said: "I don't think that I can handle another suicide, or another fight call, or another DOA."

Type of Trauma is another key variable in determining the extent to which trauma affects you. Consider the following:

- Was the trauma an act of nature or of a person?
- Were the individuals involved related?
- What was the duration of the trauma?
- What was its intensity?
- How closely does it resemble your own personal life?

Trauma induced by an individual generally causes a more severe response than that caused by an act of nature. For example, it is easier to accept your home being struck by lighting and burned than being destroyed by vandals.

In addition, the closer the relationship between the individuals involved, the more severe the trauma. For example, trauma induced by a stranger will be less severe than that induced by a spouse, a sibling, or a parent.

The trauma's duration is also significant. Your defenses wear down in time; therefore, the longer the trauma lasts, the less able you are to defend yourself against the effects.

Further, the more intense the trauma, the less you can cope. For example, while any death involves trauma, a homicide with a child victim or a death resulting from an infliction of torture will involve much more intense trauma than the death of an adult by natural causes.

Finally, the more closely the event "fits" with your own personal life, the greater the trauma is likely to be, for example deaths of small children if you have small children of your own.

Interpretation of the Traumatic Event is crucial in how you react to trauma. Generally the perceptions most strongly affecting you are blame and guilt. If you feel responsible for a trauma, you are likely to experience a much greater effect from it.

Reactions to traumatic events can help move you through the experience or prevent such progress. If you can realize that such things happen, accurately assess your role in the situation, and identify coping strategies, the experiences will be less severe.

Mediating Variables, which influence your reaction to a traumatic experience, include social support, locus of control, and use of denial. The social support for police and correctional officers is most likely to be fellow officers. They are most likely to encourage you to deny the trauma, that is, to consider traumatic experiences as simply "business as usual."

Post-Trauma Stress also includes re-victimization and secondary consequences, including that resulting from press reports and from court appearances. Officers are prime candidates for re-victimization because they have a daily potential to encounter situations considered traumatic.

Secondary consequences include the effects of trauma on other family members. If you are unable to take time for your spouse and children because you are busy dealing with trauma yourself, the family system becomes strained or disrupted: "It's like right now all my energies are going into me. I'm still trying to understand what's happened and why I feel the way I do. I just don't have the time or energy to devote towards another person."

MARITAL DIFFICULTIES

Marital difficulties are frequently related to post-traumatic stress disorder and often result in one of more of the following problems:

- Distancing from spouse.
- An emotional inability to fulfill a spousal role.
- A physical inability to fulfill a spousal role.

Distancing. You may distance yourself from your spouse as a result of a traumatic experience. You may be afraid you will be unable to control emotional responses to the traumatic incident. Such fear severely reduces your capacity to deal with others on an emotional level.

After exposure to a traumatic event, you may be unable to actively fulfill a spousal role. You may go much further than simply distancing. You may lose interest in shared activities, become emotionally unpredictable, over-controlling, or be physically unable to fulfill the spousal role:

> I think probably the most sensible explanation for me was that my wife continued down a normal path that she was on, and I went on a different path. So we became very different people. Where we started out being basically the same kind of people, I became so different that she and I no longer could really be for each other what we were in the past.

Emotional Difficulties. Emotional unpredictability includes outbursts of anger, distrust, and over-protectiveness. You may, for example, refuse to let your spouse and children go places, participate in activities, or socialize with "strangers" because of your outlook on the world. As a result of your own distrust and over-protectiveness, you may try to regulate every detail of your spouse's and children's activities.

Physical Difficulties. Physical inability to fulfill a spousal role includes much more than sexual concerns. You may physically withdraw from *any* spousal contact. You may become reluctant (or unable) to hug, kiss, or to give or receive any physical demonstrations of affection.

In conclusion, every police and correctional officer is at risk of suffering from PTSD. While the vast majority do not experience all the symptoms, each is likely to experience some.

"No, my dad never talks about the fun stuff in police work—
But then maybe that tells me something."

REFERENCES

American Psychiatric Association. (1980). *Diagnostic and Statistical Manual III.*

American Psychiatric Association. (1985). *Diagnostic and Statistical Manual of Mental Disorders* (3rd Ed.). Washington, D.C.

Burgess, A.W. and L. L.. Holmstrom. (1974). "The Rape-Trauma Syndrome." *American Journal of Psychiatry.* 131, 981-986.

Cohen, A. (1980). "I've Killed that Man Ten Thousand Times." *Police Magazine.* 3(4), 17-23.

Janoff-Bulman, R. (1985). "The Aftermath of Victimization: Rebuilding Shattered Assumptions." In C. Figley (Ed.), *Trauma and Its Wake.* New York: Brunner/Mazel.

Kijak, M. and S. Funtowics. (1982). "The Syndrome of the Survivor of Extreme Situations." *International Review of Psychoanalysis.* 9, 25-33.

Krystal, H. and W. G. Niederland. (1968). "Clinical Observations on the Survivor Syndrome." In H. Krystal (Ed.). *Massive Psychic Trauma.* New York: International Universities Press.

Parsons, E. R. (1984). "The Reparation of the Self: Clinical and Theoretical Dimensions in the Treatment of Vietnam Combat Veterans." *Journal of Contemporary Psychotherapy*, Special Issue: "PTSD: The Vietnam Veteran." Volume 14, No. 1.

Reiser, Martin and S. P. Geiger. (1984). "Police Officers as Victim." *Professional Psychology: Research and Practice.* 15,(3), 315-323.

Scott, Walter. (1908) *The Lady of the Lake.* London: MacMillan Company.

Singleton, G. and Teahan (1978). "Effects of Job-Related Stress on the Physical and Psychological Adjustment of Police Officers." *Journal of Police Science and Administration.* 6, (3), 335-361.

PART II

INDIVIDUAL MEANINGS

Stress, victimization, and post-traumatic stress disorder (PTSD) are technical concepts, but they can have an extremely personal physical and emotional effect on you.

Part I presented several of these effects. This section takes a more in-depth look at the "prices" paid by those of you who are or may become become police or corrections officers.

Loss of innocence frequently occurs when as a new officer you are exposed to people and events you didn't know existed nor ever experienced first-hand (Chapter 6).

Cynicism and negativism often follow this loss of innocence. How this happens and what it means for you personally and professionally is discussed (Chapter 7).

Loneliness and sadness play a role for officers in both the police and corrections profession. They often result from the cynical or negative outlook many officers develop (Chapter 8).

Closely related to loneliness is *isolation*. Police and correctional officers tend to isolate themselves from non-police or corrections personnel, including neighbors, old friends, and even family members (Chapter 9).

As you deal more and more with other people's pain and tragedy and with those responsible for it, you adopt ways to protect yourself from that pain. One such strategy is a *constricted and inappropriate affect*, often described as a "protective cloak" (Chapter 10).

The more involved you get in your job, the more important other officers become to you. The occupational family can take the place of brothers, sisters, your spouse, children, in fact, all those "outside" the department (Chapter 11).

Whose innocence?

Chapter 6

LOSS OF INNOCENCE

I never in a million years would have guessed there was so much violence, so much sadness, so much bitterness, so much anger, so much ugliness out there. It was beyond my comprehension. I would not have guessed it existed to the extent it does.

An advertisement for the movie *Platoon* proclaimed: "The first casualty of war is innocence." This statement captures the experience of many police and correctional officers as well. You, too, feel you lose your innocence in a combat situation lacking popular support. While combat experiences in the jungles, on our cities' streets, or in our prisons may lead to post-traumatic stress disorder (Chapter 5), they also rob you of your innocence.

You see yourself working in an us/them environment, isolated from and yet responsible for the behavior of the population you serve. Your perception of this adversarial role with citizens or inmates is accentuated by the "thou shalt not" structure of your role.

"REAL" POLICE AND CORRECTIONS WORK

Police and correction officers are often involved in maintaining order. To do so you must tell citizens that they cannot do what they would like to do, for example, drive faster or take what they consider justified revenge. You tell the inmates when to work, when to play, and when to sleep.

Police officers are hired to, and have sworn to, "uphold the law and defend the Constitution of the United States." In upholding the law, you sometimes find yourself caught where you may feel that to uphold the law and defend the Constitution is not "doing the right thing."

For example, you may be forced to help a wealthy slumlord evict a poor family from the only shelter they have. You may be called to a strike scene to "maintain order." Even though your sympathies may lie completely with the strikers, you will probably appear to be a tool of management.

COMMON MISCONCEPTIONS

Frequently misconceptions about the actual role of the police officer abound. Citizens often expect you to do things you are not permitted to do, or citizens complain when you do things you are required to do. For example, you may be called to a civil dispute where you have no authority. When you are unable to act, the citizens are outraged and vent that anger toward you.

How often you would like to have the wisdom of Solomon and threaten to divide the child (or the disputed property) to determine the rightful owner. But you cannot read minds or solve crimes without clues or without citizen cooperation. In fact, those who do cooperate with you may be labeled "snitches" or "finks."

You are often expected to stop crime on your own with no help from those you are hired to protect. This expectation probably came as a surprise to you. You were probably not accustomed to people standing and watching as others are victimized.

Most people entering police work begin with a skewed impression of what that work will be about:

I call it the TV cop syndrome. They don't see you standing on the street corner in late January directing traffic after an accident, and freezing, and thinking, "There's got to be a better way to make a living." They don't see you taking some kid to the hospital that has so much lice on him that you can't believe it. They don't see you down at the medical center with a bite in your arm from some hooker who didn't want you to arrest her and the doctors are talking about putting you in the hospital.

What they see is the TV cop doing all sorts of neat things. That's not what police work is all about.

Correctional officers are often caught between a public that cries for more humane treatment of prisoners, sweeping reforms, more prisoner rehabilitation while at the same time clamoring for more protection from criminals.

A RUDE AWAKENING

As noted, most people enter the fields of law enforcement and corrections with a naive attitude. You believe that your involvement can make the world a better place:

I think a good example of where I might have changed is that before I was employed here I was a liberal, and I was completely against capital punishment. I was completely against any kind of weapons at all. I hated guns. I'd never fired one. Since my time here, I've definitely changed.

I have no tolerance for a lot of the types of crimes that people commit, and I've noticed that as the years have gone by, I have less acceptance of that. Even though we're trained not to be judge and jury, it's hard not to do. You don't express it, but internally you really feel it.

You really just see sometimes, especially if you're a parent yourself and you're dealing with a habitual child molester. You see this person returning here time and time again and wonder why they're ever getting out of here so they can do it again. Those kind of things, and you really start losing your sense of humanity.

As you become more and more aware of the pain in the world and your inability to make things better, it becomes increasingly difficult to see the world as a good place. This creates an internal conflict involving the following logic:

- You want to make things better--but cannot.
- If you were competent, you could make things better.
- Therefore, you must not be competent.

To avoid the conclusion that you are not competent, you may unconsciously devalue the goal you cannot attain (making things better): "I think when you're younger you don't want to accept those things [that you cannot make the world a better place]. And as time goes on, you learn to accept the fact that you're ineffectual."

MEASURING COMPETENCE

The lack of specific standard measures of police or correctional success further contributes to the perception of officer ineffectiveness. Some supervisors may indicate that you are successful if you write 50 traffic citations each month, while others may measure success by the number of misdemeanor or felony arrests each month:

> That's another frustration I think officers have. You really don't know what kind of impact you have. If you're working on an assembly line and the Fords are rolling off, you can see all the cars that you're responsible for making that day. But with police work you really can't see what kind—or you don't have that measurable impact. You can't measure how you're impacting peoples' lives.

This is also true in corrections. Correctional standards may be that if all is quiet, you are doing a good job. Other supervisors may measure success inversely by the number of internal affairs complaints made against you.

It is unlikely that as a police or corrections candidate you answered that you wanted to join the ranks of law enforcement or corrections because of the high rates of divorce, alcoholism, and suicide or to become hard, cold, and cynical. While you were probably aware of the statistics, you probably also firmly believed: "It may be an occupational hazard, but it won't happen to me."

Later in your career, if asked why you entered your chosen field or what you like most about your job, you may give a variety of answers acceptable within your occupational world. But "to make the world a better place" is unlikely to be among those answers.

Your answers, in fact, may be clouded with stock responses that reveal little or nothing of your true rationales. You may answer that you like the work because you get to meet a lot of women/men, you get a check every week, or you have a good pension. But you are not likely to say you remain in your line of work for the satisfaction gained by making the world a better place. At least not until you reach the point in your career where you have moved beyond the stage of cynicism and realize that you *are* helping individuals, even though you have very little, if any, effect on the system. (This is discussed in depth in the next chapter.)

By the time you understand what your work is all about, how you are viewed by and relate to citizens and inmates, and the changes that your work has made for you, you can no longer answer with the same naivete that was natural when you entered the career.

THE "REAL" WORLD

You are unlikely to have experienced much of the seamier side of life before becoming an officer. In fact, individuals who have spent a lifetime associating with criminals, street people, and the "real" world are usually *not* hired because of this background. You may have been shocked at what went on:

> I knew there was crime, I knew there were people out there that weren't nice, but no one could tell me then about man's inhumanity to man. I didn't believe that this stuff could go on, that people could do the things that they do.

You may also have been surprised at the amount of human suffering in the world and the amount of pain people inflict on each other:

> You go into a house and you see kids that are battered and beaten and they've got nothing but piss-soaked mattresses to sleep on, no beds. You open up the refrigerator and the only thing that is in there is beer and rotting food on the stove, and it really taints ya.

A NEW AWARENESS

Not only were you probably surprised by the condition of human affairs, you were no doubt chagrined at how people treat those they're supposed to love:

> I guess I knew in a superficial way that this kind of violence existed, but I had never known the length to which someone would go to injure another person. Going to a house where a pregnant woman has been assaulted and finding her laying on the floor miscarrying because she got kicked in the stomach so many times. You wait for the ambulance and watch her miscarry and think to yourself, "That's his kid too!" I don't understand how these things happen. I don't understand how people do this stuff to each other.

Such instances bring a new awareness, an awareness you probably wished you did not have. You might be happier if you had not witnessed this human misery and cruelty: "Sometimes I wish I didn't see the things I see. It is frustrating to see things that other people don't see, can't see, and won't see."

A LOSS OF INNOCENCE

With such awareness comes loss of innocence and the realization that things can never be viewed as they once were:

I find myself very distanced from what I call the gentle people of the world, the church-goers, and the family men. They do their job and they come home and they play with their kids and they talk to their wives, and they talk to their neighbors, and whatever else they do. And they just kind of go merrily along enjoying themselves and think everything's great and it's going to be great. And sure as hell, sometimes it works out for them. It's great.

One officer described her acquisition of the special knowledge she gained as an officer as "having earned a Ph.D. in reality."

Having this special knowledge is *not* a blessing. It is like the curse of Cassandra, the figure in Greek mythology who had the gift of prophecy. But a curse was put upon her so that no one believed her. You can become extremely frustrated as illustrated in the following example:

My friends don't know what is really happening, and it is real frustrating, and I am unable to get that information out to people. I wish I could express myself better. I wish I could write articles. I wish I could get on a bandstand and just yell it out. But nobody's really listening.

Further, you may come to resent the citizen's ability to choose not to see the tragedy, misery, and suffering in this world:

We have to participate in things in order to protect the rest of the world from what's happening. If we weren't here, friends and neighbors would have to come in and take care of these situations, right? Everyone would be aware of what was happening and they'd have to be involved.

I remember the night that I watched this guy die of a heart attack in his turkey dinner. As I came out of the house, and there were red light flashing and all that stuff, I saw a neighbor drop the blinds in his living room window and go back to his Christmas Eve dinner. I thought, "It's his own neighbor, but he doesn't want to know what happened tonight—not tonight."

LOSS OF FAITH IN THE SYSTEM

The loss of innocence is also characterized by a loss of faith in the system and feelings that you have little effect on it:

> When somebody calls the police, they think something is going to happen. I know nothing is going to happen. We make our arrest and we talk to the victim, take a statement, and 99 percent of the time everybody working on a case is going to know that this guy is not going to get charged. Or he gets charged, he is not going to get anything out of it.

Another officer described similar reactions about the system not working:

> Just the day-to-day frustrations most police officers feel. They got a guy. He's going to go to jail, and he's going to go through the court system, and he's going to get slapped on the wrist. And there's some poor victim out there that's being hospitalized, and we feel that the only lumps that guy's going to get are the ones that we give him. And we know that if we punch the guy, we're going to lose our job.

It is even more obvious to correctional officers who see the failure of the system as rapists, robbers, and drug pushers keep coming back to prison time and again.

LOSS OF ENERGY

As the expectations for change fade, so does the energy to work for change. You may begin to feel there is little you can do to make things better, so why try:

> I could have been the kind of person who said, "Ah, shit. Who cares." Or, "Hey, the job is just to get a paycheck." I mean, I know coppers like that. They're only interested in the paycheck. They could care less about doing a good job.

One officer described his own loss of energy after a traumatic event:

> I guess I can compare it to the injured dog that's trying to heal. It's like right now all my energies are going into me. I'm still trying to understand what's happened and why I feel the way I feel. I just don't have the time or energy to devote towards another person.

Another said:

> I try to make sure that I have some time set aside for things that interest me instead of letting the department swallow up all my time. I know that I catch heat from the department for not being as dedicated as I was, but why should I be? What did the department give me? It's just a job. It's just a paycheck. And they would never even know the difference. And so, I don't want to let the department be number one in my life anymore, never again.

LOSS OF SELF-CONFIDENCE

When you realize you cannot change the system and cannot make things better for everyone, unfortunately, the first thing you may question is your own abilities:

> I think maybe the work fosters the idea that there is a right way and a wrong way. So I was continually looking for the right way. I believed that if you try hard enough to find a solution that you will find it. The mere belief I would find it and that I had to find the solution led to an obsession about the problem.

Another way in which the loss of innocence is experienced is in a loss of a belief in the ability to make things better within the "system." You may discover what you perceive to be significant flaws in our social system. You may have been surprised by the magnitude of social problems and your lack of ability to do much about them.

Initially the belief that the system is slow to change (if change is even possible) may not occur to you. Instead you may believe the fault lies in yourself. You feel incompetent:

> You think you're going to show this person the way. And you try and you try and, of course, you don't. After a while it sinks in. It's not going to work. These social problems are much, much greater than what we can repair. You're just there to pick up the pieces, and that's a hard lesson. Some people never learn it.

As the loss of belief in the self develops, you may begin to question your own judgment, beliefs, and values. You may question possibilities for successes and failures, often denying success and anticipating failure:

> It's like I have no confidence in my decisions any more. My self-confidence in my ability to do the job is less. I'm always second guessing myself. You know, am I doing this right? Should I be doing it differently?

LOSS OF VALUES

As you are exposed to more and more of the seamy side of life and have few successes in making any lasting change, your values may change:

> Since I came on this job, the value I place on life has certainly dropped. I used to believe that there was a worth to every life. And I don't necessarily believe that any more. I know I go on calls and a lot of people end up getting shot and stabbed and what not. I think when I first started, I felt a real sense of loss and that they were something of value. And I don't think I believe that anymore.

Another officer described this value change when he said:

> Sometimes I'm not sure what real honesty is because every-body lies. Everybody is lying. The attorneys are twisting the truth to get the guy off. And I get up there [on the witness

stand], maybe I gave him his rights and maybe I didn't, but I say I did, and it really doesn't bother me.

Loss of innocence also may affect your religious beliefs. Being exposed to so much pain and tragedy makes it difficult to believe in a benevolent God:

> I used to be really religious and was really dedicated to the church. But it doesn't seem to have any significance any more. I read the scriptures, and it will say, "God is just." But I don't see it. I'll read further, and it says, "but not here, later on." Well, I don't want to wait 'til later on. The spiritual side of my life has deteriorated.

You are also likely to see differently those who are part of the sociopolitical power structure. Dignitaries are "only human" and have "flaws," just like anyone else. You see sports heroes (maybe your own childhood idols) at their worst: drunk, fighting, and disrespectful. You see legislators and clergy with child prostitutes. You see the wealthy involved in scandal. And finally you see how the system covers it over.

A NEW VIEW OF YOUR COLLEAGUES

You also discover that your peers are people with human frailties and human desires—the very same ones you are frequently criticized for or are required to find as faults in others. You see them drunk, fighting (perhaps with their spouses), and even abusing the power given them by virtue of their occupation.

LOSS OF HUMANITY

You may even experience a loss of your own humanity. It may become extremely difficult to be gentle, caring, tender, and nurturing. These feelings create vulnerability, forcing you to feel the pain of those you work with. So you devise various shields to protect yourself:

I think I create some distance and some hesitancy. It is easier. It is harder to let go and let that curtain down. I know sometimes when I'm off duty and in a situation where it is mildly confrontational or where I need to be assertive, I will put on this mask of being a police officer. I can be assertive that way, and it feels like a different part of me that I drop when I am off duty. I try to, but it is not too far away from me. It is still there–a hesitancy to let yourself be known, to be vulnerable with somebody, to be emotionally intimate, to share things. It is hard to do that.

LOSS OF THE PAST

Along with the loss of innocence may come a certain loss of your past. You seem to have lost your friends and "the person you used to be." No one is as he or she was before becoming an officer. Your life loses continuity, and you may be unable to connect the person you used to be with the person you have become.

I still say I have them [old friends], but I never see them. So I lost them all. Seems to me you lose them. If you think about it, you lose a whole lot of things when you do this job. You gain some things–new friends and all that. But everything you had in the past you might as well forget about, cause it all changed for me. It's all gone.

It's all gone.

THEN: "When I grow up I wanna be just like him."

NOW: "Listen lady... If you want somebody to go catch a crook, call Joe Friday."

Even the bars are designed to keep people out.

Chapter 7

CYNICISM

I can take this uniform off and put it in my locker when I go home, but I've only got one brain. It's the brain I brought with me the first day I came to work, and it's the same brain I got everyday. That brain has been programmed to be negative. I don't trust you because you might hurt me. I don't trust you because you're standing out in front of that store because you're a lookout. You're a bad guy until I know otherwise. That's what I learned, and for the last twenty-eight years that's what I've practiced.

Cynicism is a major price you may pay to be a police officer or a correctional officer. It is a stage you experience as you mature in your occupation. It is in this context that cynicism is discussed in this chapter.

As you progress through your career, you follow a general developmental pattern, and your outlook is likely to change with each pattern.

THE ROOKIE STAGE

During the rookie stage you are relatively naive and have not seen what the "real world" is like. You are very concerned with fitting in with the other officers. You want to look, sound, act, and think like a *real* cop or *real* guard. You may spend hours working on your equipment (shining shoes and brass) trying to make it look sharp, yet also doing anything you can to make the equipment look as used as that of the seasoned veterans.

During this stage being an officer is just about the most important thing in your life. To be a "real" cop or guard, you try to act like you know what you are doing, sound like you don't believe in anything or anyone, and let everyone know that this world is on a rapid downhill spiral.

As a rookie you may talk a tough game, but are still not sure what the "rules" are or how the game is *really* played. You are still frequently shocked by what you see.

FROM ROOKIE TO CYNIC

Before you know it, you've become a cynic. During this stage you "*know*"* that the system doesn't work because you have had numerous experiences with the system's failures. You've arrested the same failures time after time only to see them released, sometimes before you have finished the paper work. Corrections officers see the same inmates return to prison countless times.

You may have seen the delinquents you arrested when they were kids grow up to be arrested as adults and *their* children arrested as delinquents or the inmates' children become inmates:

> You see the same names pop up over and over again. The same assholes committing the same crimes, or the same families for that matter. Ya got some families out in my district here where the guys that are thirty some years old. Now all of a sudden, little twelve-year-olds are starting to get into it, and I'm thinking, "Christ, I'll be fifty some years old and these guys will be twenty-five and I'll still be chasing them around for the next twelve years." And then their brothers and sisters will get into it too. So the same names keep popping up all the time. That in itself is frustrating.

---

*The word "know" is used here to convey a strength of conviction. It has little to do with reality, but, rather, is the officer's perception of reality.

One of the first emotions you experience as a rookie is disappointment, partially resulting from your inability to "make a difference" because you have no super powers.

Disappointment. New police and corrections officers quickly learn that they are not much different from other people. They come in all shapes, colors, and sizes. Some are good, some are bad, but most are a little bit of both—human. Most care about the people they serve, some don't. Yet all wear the same uniform.

As a new officer, you soon experience disappointment with yourself and others. You are disappointed with yourself because you do not seem to be doing the job. There is more crime now than when you began your career. You are disappointed with others because no one else seems to care if the job gets done.

One officer described learning that police are human when he described a conversation with a partner: "You bastard, you're drunk, at seven o'clock in the morning." And his partner replied: "I don't know how that happened. I stopped drinking at four."

Negatives and Negativism. Police officers constantly deal with the negative. You take crime reports, accident reports, help the sick and injured, and investigate death scenes. You deal with people who are victims or criminals--sometimes both. Correctional officers serve a population consisting entirely of convicted criminals, even though many frequently proclaim their innocence.

You see the world as a place of hurt, anger, sadness, and fear. This is what you come to expect. This is the way the world is.

> We go down one night on a bogus call. My partner and I got out, and we were immediately surrounded. If I hadn't thought to bring a portable radio with us, well, they probably would have had our scalps.

> It tends to make a person prejudiced because you don't see the good black people. You don't see the good white people. All you see is the shit.

Often you cannot separate the negatives at work from the rest of your life, even when you're doing "fun" things.

> I would like to be able to go and enjoy the circus. But no. On the way there I'm looking at all the "dirtbags" on the street. I think "I'm going to the circus." Then I wonder how many people in the circus are beating their wives.

General Lack of Trust. One aspect of this negative attitude is displayed in the lack of trust you show for others. You have difficulty trusting anyone and assume that each new person is going to hurt you, until proven otherwise:

> I think I'm cynical of relatives, friends, everybody. That I don't think goes away. I'm not willing to bare my soul, and I'm on guard even with people that I really shouldn't be on guard with. You should accept them for what they are until they prove that they're something different. And I don't. I think that's the job. How do I want to say it? It's just part of the job. You just don't trust people.

This "burden of proof" is often unreasonable because you usually don't believe the proof anyway. People are rarely able to provide sufficient proof to convince you of their innocence. No matter how much proof is provided, your mind is made up and you "don't want to be confused by facts." You have been lied to so often that you accept little, if anything, on faith.

Those who suffer most often from these demands are your family. Children are often the most unfortunate victims of this distrust. They need to prove almost everything to you who need to be officer at home too:

> I think I take it home all the time. Probably to the degree that I've said done some things with my family, including my children, where I've been distrustful and they've almost had to prove their innocence before I'll accept it, which is not healthy in my mind.

This distrust is, of course, an essential "survival mechanism" while on duty. But you may develop an inability to trust either *on or off* duty, unable to separate on-duty survival mechanisms from off-duty family and social life. Clearly, this is more than "attitude." It is a way of life and encompasses your entire world. It is caused and supported by the tension experience in your work. In this way it is profound.

On-the-job Disappointments. Professionally, persons you thought needed help or may have given a break to, have turned out to be most unappreciative of your help. For example, an inebriated person you gave a ride home complains that you were rude or abusive. The inmate whom a guard has confided in or trusted a bit is invariably the one who takes most serious advantage of you.

Personal Disappointments. Cynical officers have learned about disappointment and are unwilling to risk further pain. The axiom "Better to have loved and lost than never to have loved at all" is not always true. Rather, you hold to the axiom: "The one who expects nothing is never disappointed." At this point in your career, you may find the world rather bleak. To view the world as dreary place with little room for joy, happiness or hope for a better future is part of the personal toll of cynicism.

LOSS OF VALUES, FAIRNESS, AND JUSTICE.

For a time during the cynical stage, you may lose your belief in such core values as truth, honesty, justice, fair-play, and religion as a belief system. Personal and social justice are no longer yardsticks for determining what is good or true.

It becomes increasingly difficult to enforce the laws fairly and impartially when you *know* that a criminal with enough money may very well walk away from the crime. If convicted (and you believe that in itself unlikely), the criminal will be sentenced to probation by a lenient judge or remain free on bond awaiting an appeal. And correctional officers may see influential inmates wielding just as much power "inside" as when on the "outside."

You also see others becoming rich in the world of drugs—gaining their wealth through the misery and dependence of those to whom they peddle their merchandise. You see these drug barons reap their spoils from a culture that seems to encourage a few moments of pleasure for a lifetime of pain. You also see these same people encouraging children to become mini-barons and deal drugs to friends.

It is personally difficult to arrest someone for stealing a loaf of bread when a business executive, who has cheated the government of millions in taxes, is walking around free. from

These lessons teach daily that the world is *not* fair and just. You see this more than most people because you are constantly personally involved with unfairness and injustice. In fact, to many citizens you symbolize unfairness and injustice because you are the enforcement arm of what may be systematic unfairness and injustice.

Personal Disillusionment. You probably grew up believing in "justice" and "fair-play." Undoubtedly, you were taught to respect the law and the rights of others.

You come to perceive these suppositions as false and begin to build on disappointments. The Golden Rule: "Do unto others as you would have others do unto you" is replaced with: "Do unto others before they do unto you."

You learn that you can count on no one except perhaps your partner. You are disappointed by the "system," the administration, and the "do-gooders" of the world who just don't realize what needs to be done to make the world better.

Disillusionment with the System. Police and correctional officers want criminals to be apprehended, convicted, and punished. Citizens seem to want constitutional rights, cost effectiveness, plea bargains, and "rehabilitation" for offenders. Police and correctional officers are left with the frustration of ineffectiveness and the painful task of dealing with victims and criminals, knowing there will be no justice.

One officer described his feelings about the system after his daughter had had an encounter with an exposer:

My wife wanted to run right over and talk to his [the suspect's] parents. I said let's not even waste our time. I don't' want to get into a big hassle. Why don't we just burn down their garage or something else? The woman [suspect's mother] said your daughter was at the [municipal] swimming pool so she was 50% wrong to start with. They're not going to do anything about it. Nothing is going to change. I just don't even bother to call the cops anymore.

You come to believe that Lady Justice is not blindly impartial, but instead, blindly ignorant and incompetent. The shattering of these values, beliefs, and expectations leads to a sadness and a loss of hope that anything better can or will occur. The emptiness inside is often painful. To relieve that pain you may just quit caring—about your job, about trying to help people, and even about yourself. You just put in your time, but do not exert any real effort to do a good job.

You withdraw from those you are hired to help as well as from those who may help you. You are rewarded for your lack of effort with continued employment and perhaps even a promotion because you "don't rock the boat." You receive few complaints from Internal Affairs and are not in a high profile position. While the citizens are not getting the service they are paying for, the department is not needing to respond to complaints about you.

A Change in Job Perspective. As you stop caring, you can no longer retain your self-esteem in knowing you do a good job. This is just another "spoke" in your "wheel of depression."

Another way you may respond is to stop caring about the "system" and decide to do the job *in spite of* the administration and courts. You may take "shortcuts" and circumvent the Constitution as well as department policies and procedures to "get the job done" as you see it needs to be done.
You are branded a "trouble maker" and may find it difficult to continue in police or correctional work.

By not caring or by not working within the established framework, however, you create a vicious cycle. You make an arrest based on illegally obtained evidence and think you have done a good job because you have gotten another criminal off the streets. When the case is dismissed because of illegally obtained evidence, you see another failure of the system. You may blame the prosecutor or the judge or both, but you seldom see that your shortcuts were the reason the criminal is back on the streets.

Officers vs. Citizens and the System. To compound the matter, you may become the focus of civil lawsuits by those found not guilty or by inmates who feel they have been dealt with inappropriately. Again, you see few rewards for your work. The attorney representing you may settle out of court, indicating that they believe you to be at fault. Or a judge or jury may determine that you were at fault.

While most agencies and some officers carry insurance to protect against civil damage, juries can and do award punitive damages which you are often required to pay personally. In your mind this is just another lack of reward for what you feel is necessary to protect citizens.

"Do-Gooders" and Lambs. Cynical officers see as "naive" those who look on the bright side, the people who believe in the intrinsic value of life and the basic goodness of people. You tend to label these people as "fuzzy-headed do-gooders."

An old yellowed piece of paper (source and author unknown) posted on the wall of a roll call room described the police officer's perception of their role:

> The policeman, he told us, is a mercenary: Society tries to make us out to be the Jolly Green Giants of the community. We're not. We're the barbed wire separating the wolves from the lambs.

This seems to be even more true of correctional officers as they protect the "lambs" from thousands of victimizers.

Yet these "lambs," *not* officers, serve as jurors. These people must convict the criminals you have apprehended. Frequently you feel jurors are too trusting and believing, giving criminals another chance to commit crimes.

Jurors don't see criminals in the same light you do. By the time criminals get to trial, they are cleaned up, are polite and courteous, and are represented by counsel. You may be further frustrated when you testify that you *eye-witnessed* a suspect commit a crime and the criminal denies it and is believed by the judge or jury.

You may have followed all procedures and done everything properly, to no avail. The judge or jury believe the criminal instead of you. This is frustrating and discourages continued good work. You know you have told the truth and have not been believed. Again, you may wonder: "Why am I doing this?"

Jurors don't see criminals in the same light as do correctional officers either. Citizens do not have to interact with these criminals in all their vulgarity as they manipulate each other and the system.

Second-Class Citizens. Many officers see themselves as going through a lot to help the community, yet they also see themselves being treated as second-class citizens:

> I guess over the years I've become more cynical because of these invasions of [our] rights. Basically it's our job to uphold the law, but yet we are not afforded the opportunity to receive the protection from the same law that we provide to other people.

Under what has been called the "Garrity Rule," police officers are *required* to answer allegations of misconduct during an internal affairs investigation or face losing their jobs. Every citizen has the "right to remain silent" *except* police officers. You are required to answer to any allegations. And your answers are likely to appear on the front page of tomorrow's newspaper. You have little right to privacy. Your alleged mistakes are news that sell papers at the expense of you and your family.

If newspaper headlines falsely describe you as making a "brutal arrest" or as being a "crooked cop," the effect on you and your family is devastating. If correctional officers are described as brutal or accused of maintaining inhumane conditions for inmates, the effect on you and your family is equally traumatic. Even though you are later found entirely blameless, your reputation has been seriously damaged. Your integrity is much more subject to question than that of the general public.

In addition, when you are cleared, that's not usually headlines. The exoneration may, just may, find space hidden in the middle or back of the paper.

You may also become cynical because you see yourself as doing what you can to keep citizens safe. This means you must take on danger yourself. Yet you believe you are often placed in danger and receive little or no support:

> I've even had contracts out on me and had to have other cops follow me home. That changes you. I mean you get hard. You've got to get hard. I was taking a squad car home with a shotgun sitting next to me.

MOVING ON–THE THIRD STAGE

After you experience the cynicism of the second stage, in the third stage you begin to realize you *are* making a difference. You may not be saving the world, but your finally realize that people do care and many appreciate all that you go through.

You begin to sort through the negative and find some hope in your world. You find rewards when a small child says, "Thank you, Officer," after you have helped her find where she lives and brought her home or have come to her school and taught the children about bicycle safety. You find a reward when an inmate who is being released says, "Thank you" and tells you that you have made a difference and that he or she is determined to not commit more crimes–and doesn't. These become rewards for you. You realize you have made things better for a few of those whose lives you have touched.

In this third stage you become more objective and realistic. In the cynical stage, you may think you're a realist. But when you reach the third stage you realize you *are* helping make the world a better place. Finally, you begin to accept things and become involved in activities outside of police or correctional work: "As I get older, my off-duty time has become very, very precious. We've usually got so many things going, especially with two teenage kids, that work frustrations are ignored."

After you have progressed through the cynical stage, your life is more in focus. But before this stage is reached, many other "prices" may be paid. These are discussed in the following chapters.

"Listen kid, don't believe nothing people tell ya!"

Who's there for him?

Chapter 8

LONELINESS

I am the loneliest man in the world, the loneliest man in the world. I still had friends, still had people that cared for me, but I was lonely. Nobody was in there with me where it was really terrible.

Police and correctional officers are often alone. You work alone, intervene in people's lives alone, and may make life-and-death decisions alone. You are trained to work alone and become used to being alone and to working alone. Yet *alone* and *lonely* are not the same. While the aloneness of such work is to be expected, it need not be painful (lonely).

You are trained in specific tactics to ensure your safety *because* you are alone. You are trained to deal with people in specific ways *because* you are alone. To work alone and make life-or-death decisions alone in a split second is part of your work.

It is what happens *after* this aloneness or the results of things done alone that lead to the loneliness. The aloneness is physical. Being lonely is emotional. It results from several factors, some external, others internal.

EXTERNAL CAUSES OF LONELINESS

Among the external causes of loneliness are criticism from the public, lack of support, and citizens' fear of the polices' power to arrest or the correctional officers' duty to incarcerate.

Criticism. You are frequently criticized for your decisions. Yet in almost all cases, the critics were not present when the decision was made. They do not have the information you had on which to base the decision. Also, they have none of the personal involvement which you have.

People standing back criticizing your decisions have no personal investment. And they have all the time necessary to discover relevant facts and weigh them carefully before making a decision. They don't have to deal with four screaming women, five hysterical kids, and three angry men while they deliberate. Neither are they surrounded by a dozen threatening inmates while they "deliberate."

In addition, critics may never have had to make decisions about other people's lives. Yet these same people are often critical of your response in a situation where they cannot begin to comprehend all the ramifications.

As the saying goes, "Don't comment until you have walked a mile in the other person's shoes." You are often forced to justify your split-second decisions to people who have days, even weeks or months to examine the same facts you looked at, realizing that they may well come to a different decision.

Civilian Review Boards. You may be required to stand before a civilian commission or review board to justify your actions. If a complaint is made against you, it often seems no one takes your side. This constant review and the potential for criticism further contribute to your feelings of loneliness.

In reaction to one city's proposal to establish a civilian review board, an opponent wrote a letter to the editor (J.I.S. 1990, p.16A) questioning who would be qualified to serve on such a board:

> Has the applicant ever faced a life-and-death situation requiring split-second decisions? Has the applicant ever witnessed the murder of a fellow colleague? Is the applicant familiar with the "ugly" as well as the "beautiful" neighborhoods of...?" [city deleted]

The letter writer feels these qualifications are necessary and ends the letter with the question: "How many citizens can fulfill those qualifications, much less, even want to?"

Officers in that city were opposed to such a board, fearing citizens did not understand their job or such police concepts as "command presence" and "verbal force" sometimes used in high risk encounters. The public often does not consider that there may be no time for "please" and "thank you."

According to one police sergeant (Diaz, 1990, p.7B): "We're dealing with street people out there. They talk street, we talk street. But the street doesn't run up into the City Council."

Another sergeant, a spokesperson for the department's Emergency Response Unit, said: "Walk a mile in our combat boots before you judge us."

The world where correctional officers work is also unique. How many people can understand criminals, develop a "working relationship" with them, and feel what it is like to be locked up with over one thousand people who don't like (hate?) you?

Lack of Support. Once you make your decisions, not only are you often criticized, you must live with your decisions, often with little or no support from others. This can cause a transition from "alone" to "lonely."

Your decisions can lead to promotion or to disciplinary action. There can be favorable results in criminal court (a conviction) or damaging results in civil court (a judgment against you).

The Supreme Court has been described as the embodiment of judicial wisdom, and yet you must instantaneously meet the criteria that these jurists will spend months establishing after you have acted.

Arrest and Incarceration Power. While officers are often the victims of Monday morning quarterbacks, they are not helpless. In fact, you possess an incredible amount of power. As noted by Blumberg and Niederhoffer (1976, p.10):

Most of us do not fully comprehend the implications of the awesome power that the police possess in their exercise of discretion to arrest. In a simple situation involving a defendant of modest means, arrest may cause loss of job, a period of detention, the indignities of being fingerprinted and photographed, immeasurable psychic pain, at least several court appearances—and finally the expenditure of many hundreds of dollars for bail and a lawyer.

This arrest power is like the Sword of Damocles, in that you have the authority to intervene in other people's lives for their "safety and protection," yet you intervene most often by telling people "thou shall not." Police authority encourages citizens to maintain a greater distance from you because everyone has done something they could be "caught" for.

Correctional officers may well be "tainted" by the inmates they work with. It is difficult for the public to see guards as warm, compassionate, and tender and to still perceive that they are capable of doing their job. It is easier to imagine you as hard, cold, and efficient, but certainly not as someone with whom you'd want to be close friends with.

INTERNAL FACTORS

Loneliness results not only from external factors, but also from internal factors, some of which you've already briefly looked at.

Inability to Trust. You've heard, "It's lonely at the top." That's because those at the top must make decisions that affect other people's lives. Officers not only make such decisions daily, they also take the initiative to see that the decisions are put into effect. It becomes lonely because you need to be constantly vigilant in dealing with people.

You may feel compelled to stand alone because you don't know if a certain friendship may put you in a compromising position. Again, you find it difficult to be close to people because you don't know what others want or expect from you.

Fear of Investing. An inability to trust often leads to a sense of loneliness and sadness. You may experience a sense of loss, uselessness, and frustration because you are so alone. You wish you could trust, but seem unwilling to risk hurt or disappointment. This is one result of the cynicism described in Chapter 7 and is directly related to it:

> If you show a little weakness, they will come down on you, and you'll just never live it down. So you say, "OK, the hell with it. Screw it, I didn't want to do it anyway." You protect yourself in every way.

This fear of investing in others, of giving yourself over to another, is experienced as being vulnerable. To give yourself over to the control of another risks being misused and hurt. This unwillingness to risk relationships keeps you apart from others and alone. You are entrapped and isolated by your own lack of courage to risk hurt, thereby becoming lonely.

You may feel you have no one to talk with, no one to understand how you feel and what you have been experiencing. Since you know others won't understand, it seems useless to try.

Special Knowledge. Special knowledge and ways of relating to the world may also leave you lonely. In his fictional writings based on the reality of police life, Joseph Wambaugh (1972) writes:

> But they did have a secret which seemed to unite them more closely than normal friendship and that was the knowledge that they *know* things, basic things about strength and weakness, courage and fear, good and evil, especially evil....
>
> Police see a hundred percent of criminality. We see non-criminals and real criminals who are involved in crime. We see witnesses to crimes and victims of crimes and we see them during and right after and we see victims sometimes before the crimes occur and we know they're going to be victims, and we see perpetrators. We can't do a damned thing about it even though we know through our experience. We *know*.

This knowledge contributes to your loneliness because there is no one to tell. You often feel only you have this special *knowledge*.

Others don't want to know the things police and correctional officers know. This relates to the loss of innocence described earlier because you are lonely in the knowledge that robbed you of your naivete.

Distancing. You are not encouraged to discuss your feelings with others:

> Most of my friends have always been a little bit leery of me. You get too close and they back up. They don't want to hear really hard things, emotional things. If you said, "Gee, I really feel terrible, I feel like I could sit down and cry if I knew how" or "I'm really having a bad time, would you just spend some time with me and talk to me and be nice to me?" It just drives them away. They don't want to get that tight I guess, men in particular.

Therefore, you don't express your feelings and come to have little, if any, meaningful emotional contact with others:

> I go home and it's like there's nothing there. I have no real reason to go home other than it's there. I spend a lot of time there. I'll sit and watch TV. I try to stay busy with little odd jobs and things. I don't think there's any way that when I'm away from this job that I can function normally.
>
> I've tried getting out to sporting events and functions like that, just to see them, to be with people, and even there I feel out of place and alone.

Lack of Intimacy. Closely related to distancing are inabilities to become intimate with or committed to others. You may say you have closer relations with strangers than with your spouse and children.

Ironically, you want emotional distance between yourself and those with whom you are in a long-term relationship. The closer the person, the colder the relationship. This strategy protects both you and your significant others.

It is logical that if you cannot communicate emotions to those you are committed to, the pain is not communicated either. Consequently, you experience no guilt because you have not shared pain with those with whom you are close. You have protected them:

> I kept my wife and family completely separate from the department, and I never shared anything with them at all. I always thought that my wife and kids don't have to know about all that crap down there.

Another officer said: "You just don't want to take that stuff home. She's working, and she's got other problems."

Involvement with Strangers. With a stranger, you have no such worries or constraints. You can end relationships at any point:

> I'm very lonely. In fact, I'm working on that. I've been working on that for a couple of years. It's a big issue. That loneliness when you have got yourself entrenched in your place and nobody can come in. When it gets so bad that you can't stand it anymore, then you go out and look for somebody to come in and play with you for a while.
>
> And that is, of course, a stranger. And that's where the other involvements come in. It's got to be another woman who quote, understands you, or will let you talk and play and be who you want to be.

There is little risk, and the consequences of sharing do not rebound. This is one-way giving. It is an unloading, not dialogue or a mutual relationship.

If you begin to feel guilty because you are causing pain in others by living as a hurt being, you can simply leave. Leaving is a way to escape the pain confirmed by being close to another.

You are allowed to "talk and play and be who you want to be." This is important because you may not be sure who you are. All your past seems to be gone. As the officer said in

Chapter 6: "Everything you had in the past you might as well
forget about, 'cause it all changed for me. It's all gone."

This loss of a past contributes to your loneliness, as do
internal changes that take place:

> I was afraid of myself. I'd just become somebody else when
> I finally looked at it, and that isn't what I wanted to be. I
> didn't like it. Everything that I did turned into a real
> life-threatening situation. I put myself in those situations.
> I don't know what it was, just doing crazy things. I was just
> doing crazy things.

Intimacy with strangers is pseudo-intimacy. You may very
well relate painful feelings and experiences, often to manipulate others. When you tell of sad experiences, it may be to
get strangers to feel sorry for you. There is no display of
weakness when talking with strangers because they are never
allowed to know who you *really* are.

The risk of infecting a stranger with your pain is of little
importance because the stranger is really of no great importance to you. In all likelihood you want the person to remain
a stranger. If you allow someone to penetrate your armor, the
stranger becomes too close.

The risk of contamination from your pain increases as the
relationship becomes closer. Therefore, it is important that
strangers remain strangers. If confronted about how you are
living a lie, and you are lying now, you can simply end the
relationship—and usually do.

Inability to Talk. If you are committed to a relationship, you
are called on to be honest, and this you cannot do easily.
Many officers cannot talk about things important to them,
their fears, hopes, disappointments. Perhaps the difficulty lies
in combining intimacy and honesty rather than in combining
intimacy and commitment.

Officers have said there was "nobody inside with me where
it was really terrible." But that seems to be because you do
not live in a way that allows you to give of yourself and to let
yourself be touched by others:

It's pretty hard for a person to get any help when they don't want it, and I don't think I wanted it. No, it wasn't that I didn't want it. I didn't know there was any to get. I thought it was a lost cause.

WALLS

You may have seen so many other people touched in painful ways that you refuse to share of yourself with anyone because of a fear of getting hurt. Your fears may be so strong that even your spouse cannot get inside because you erect walls to keep everyone out. Such walls can be built in several ways.

You may say that commitment in a relationship creates a barrier to intimacy. You may say that others cannot get inside where the pain is because it is unacceptable to admit any experience of pain within the framework in which you are enmeshed. Or you may say strangers don't get inside where the pain is because they don't get inside where things are "real."

These are half-truths, however, and must be incorporated in the greater truth: *the sharing of self may be too frightening to be allowed.*

You experience loneliness largely because of the trauma you are exposed to. It is difficult for you to explain what your experiences mean to anyone who has not been involved in similar experiences:

The smell of it [a DOA call], too, if you can experience that, then you remember that forever. I think it would really be nice if everybody could experience something like that to really get a total understanding of what we go through. I mean, they read in the paper that Joe Blow got blown away, or this guy got stabbed or something, and all they're doing is reading words. Again, they can't totally comprehend it. I mean not that I would expect them to go out and do that, but what they read in the paper and what I see in reality is a whole different ball game, totally different.

Again, they know that there's problems, but being in the profession that I am in and seeing it first hand, it's a lot different, a lot different.

Correctional officers live alone also. It is impossible for someone not involved to understand the potential for trauma you live with or the reality of the trauma you experience.

Since you generally do not discuss the affective components of such situations, you must deal with them alone, behind your walls. Again, aloneness leads to loneliness. As you become more convinced that no one can understand what it is like, you try less frequently to convey these feelings. With the increasing belief in the futility of expressing the affective components of such trauma, comes increasing loneliness.

One officer described a hope for an end to his loneliness: "Someday, when I get the courage up or whatever I need to do to get out and get out of this, meet people and get out of this loneliness, then I will."

Until that happens the walls will remain and the loneliness will continue.

REFERENCES

Blumberg, A. and A. Niederhoffer. (1976). In Abraham S. Blumberg and Arthur Niederhoffer (Eds.). *The Ambivalent Force*. Springfield: Charles C. Thomas.

Diaz, K. "Police Fear Review Board's Ignorance of Life on the Street." *Star Tribune*. January 24, 1990, p. 7B.

S., J. I. "Civilian Review Board." *Star Tribune*. January 24, 1990, p. 16A.

Wambaugh, Joseph. *The New Centurions*. (1972) Boston: Little Brown.

"That's great . . . Another night at home and all that's on are cop shows."

All alone in this little box on top of a wall.

Chapter 9

ISOLATION

I wasn't close to anybody because I saw myself being in a situation where nobody knew what it was like for me and nobody would understand even if I told them. I thought I was pretty different in my pain and agony. I wasn't close to anybody now that I think about it.

Isolation is described as the setting apart of others or detachment from the social or cultural system of interaction. Police and correctional officers are isolated for many reasons. You are isolated because you choose to be or because you *need* to be. In either case, you tend not to become involved with mainstream society. This isolation becomes a seed bed for the growth of cynicism.

Isolation, in this context, is both a physical and emotional distancing from others. You may distance yourself from others without necessarily experiencing the pain of loneliness. Isolation is often a protective device to maintain ego integrity. It protects you from having to face the challenges of the occupation (e.g., the responsibility to continuously protect or control others).

The experience and feelings of being alone may lead to *physical isolation.* You feel that aloneness as an emotional barrier to social interaction. The result is psychological and social isolation reinforced by physical distance.

Psychological isolation originates in your perception that you are, or need to be, alone. Based on this perception, you may withdraw from most meaningful social contacts:

I feel separate from people, different from people, out of
step with them. There is part of me that still has some of
the common attitudes, viewpoints, hobbies, and activities.
Then there is this break at some point where my personal
viewpoints are so different, it separates me. I need my alone
time. It is something I don't really choose. I need it, so I
don't choose it, but I wish I didn't need so much time alone
to recharge.

NATURE OF THE WORK AS A CAUSE OF ISOLATION

Several aspects of isolation are inherent in police work
including single officer car patrol, pressure to make instanta-
neous life-and-death decisions while working alone, and police
duties in general. These areas contribute to and support an
ethical self-reliance and isolate you from the majority of the
non-police world.

Modern police methods enhance individual isolation. The
"beat cop" is seldom deployed because of the financial
inefficiency of such patrol. "Beat cops" were integrated into
the daily life of their neighborhoods and community. They
knew almost everyone on their beats, knew their children's
names, knew how old they were, and certainly knew who the
trouble-makers were. They interacted daily with the good and
the bad people on their beats. They spoke with both the good
people when they were not being victimized and with the bad
when they were not victimizing.

The Squad Car. Today, however, your patrol car isolates you
from the community, protecting you from the rain, cold and
heat, as well as from those you perceive as dangerous. You
have little or no contact with citizens other than about
police-related matters, which are almost exclusively negative:

> Just the very nature of your work alone, creates that sensa-
> tion [of being alone or isolated], or it starts it out. It's the
> fact that you're *encapsulated* in this car, and you're driving
> along. Usually the windows are rolled up because you're
> moving, so you're in this *steel cocoon*.

As you drive around in your squad car with the windows up, in the winter to stay warm, in the summer to stay cool, you are isolated in your "cocoon." Cocoons, however, serve not only to isolate caterpillars as they change to butterflies, but to protect them from predators as well.

Also, the radio isn't tuned to music. Almost everything you hear is clamoring to share pain with you. It is a world with more of the darker shades of gray and few rainbows.

Distrust of Authority. The very existence of your authority tends to isolate you from society. Police officers have the authority to make immediate life-or-death decisions. A common reaction to such authority is distrust. Because of this distrust, you may further isolate yourself from society.

You are also often "second-guessed" by superiors, the public, and the media. This "second-guessing" feeds isolation. You expect little support from the public, the media, and sometimes even from your superiors. This distance creates a self/others dichotomy, in which other officers are usually included with the self, but that self is isolated from others—the familiar *us vs. them* view.

Correctional officers, also, are isolated because you are to an extent outside the mainstream of society. You tend to be separated from the rest of the world because of the nature of your work. The inmates are in prison, separated from society for the good of that society. Yet your separation as a correctional officer is just as complete.

The lack of trust builds in a prison setting and serves to isolate you further:

> I think the thing that really throttles me is when you believe somebody, you've talked before, it's still inmate-officer, but you feel that you have a little rapport. And then you find out that it was a bunch of shit. He was shuckin' and jivin'. And it irritates you. And then, of course, the next time that you deal with that situation, your attitude is different.

STEREOTYPES

You may also feel isolated because you wear a uniform, and the public does not deal with you as an individual. The person inside the uniform is nonexistent. The entity is "the police" with all the attendant affect the stereotype generates. You are blamed or lauded *not* on individual merit, but on citizens' stereotypes of police. This varies greatly from community to community, but seldom provides individual recognition or positive feedback.

Most people learn about correctional officers from what they see on television or in the movies. It's not big news if you go out of your way to make things better for an inmate, but it's "prime time" if charges of corruption or brutality are leveled against you. This is big news and gets extensive coverage. Movies such as *Lockup,* continue to foster this stereotype of correctional officers as corrupt, stupid, and brutal. It shows you as a pawn of a corrupt system with no personal values or moral integrity.

These stereotypes discourage the public from reaching beyond the uniform to get to know you as an individual and, thus, continue to keep you isolated:

> I think that when I go some place, the people I meet perceive me differently than if I worked at 3M. I think it has to do with a lot of people's perception of what my job is like. A lot of people think it's like the movies, the old Cagney movies, that the guards have big sticks, that they're big people, that they don't think for themselves, that they're into a muscle game with the inmates. The average person does not have any concept of what goes on here in this institution.

GUARDIANS OF MORALITY

You are further isolated from society because you are assigned the duties of a "guardian angel," directing public morals. The public seldom likes it.

Crimes of morality, such as prostitution, for example, are often called *victimless crimes,* and vary greatly from state to state. You may incur public hostility by enforcing such laws.

You are required to enforce laws regulating areas the majority of the public often does *not* necessarily want regulated. You are told to make sure that any gambling is done so the state gets its share. Or to make sure that any liquor dispensed is done according to the rules, maybe not before 8:00 am or on Sunday.

Another area in which you incur hostility is enforcing traffic regulations. Everyone agrees traffic enforcement is necessary and saves lives, but no one wants it enforced on them. On the other hand, if you do *not* enforce traffic laws rigidly, groups dedicated to strict enforcement raise a public outcry. Traffic accidents also increase proportionately.

OFFICIAL ROLES AND THEIR EFFECT ON SOCIAL LIFE

Ironically, even enforcing the most insignificant law can isolate you. On one particular night, it was my duty to close a city park at 10:00 p.m. and lock the gate after everyone had left. I noticed one car remained. As I pulled up behind the car, I saw the windows were heavily fogged. I thought the hour too late to use the siren, so I turned on my red lights to indicate to those in the car it was time to leave.

After a few moments nothing had happened, so I approached the driver's side of the car and knocked on the window. When the driver rolled down the window, I recognized him and also could see he had no clothes on. As I looked further into the car, I recognized the passenger too, and she was also naked. Further, I also knew the man's wife and the woman's husband—both couples socially.

About two weeks later, my wife and I were at a party and these two couples were also there. Both couples left within 15 minutes of my arrival. I obviously made them very uncomfortable. We *never* socialized again.

Another officer tells of a neighborhood friend with whom he went fishing frequently and regularly. That neighbor attempted suicide, and the officer was dispatched to assist. After that call, they *never* fished together again.

In both cases professional duties created a barrier that prevented us from interacting on a level of friendship with the people we served. Every officer has stories of being isolated because of official duties:

> When I go with a group to a party, I tell my friends I don't want it brought up what I do for a living. Generally the people I hang around with assume the police are wrong anyway. And so if you say you're a police officer all they do is tell you about, "Oh well, I got this ticket..." "I saw these police beating a person..." or whatever. And they always assume that the police are wrong.

This isolation may mean you do not acknowledge you are an officer when you are not working. Or it may mean you withdraw from social contact:

> I know over the years I have gotten real isolated. Most of the time I prefer to just sit home. Three or four years ago we bought a VCR, and I don't ever leave the house. If I am off duty, I would just as soon sit at home and watch the movies, usually movies about cops or Rambo.

Even normal work hours of others can be very isolating. When you are off, either during the week or during the day, most people are at work. It is often difficult to connect with non-police friends simply because of differing schedules.

An officer described a situation where his neighbor would threaten to send her children to his home for discipline if they were "bad." These children were being taught that police officers are for punishment, not help. This certainly helped to isolate the officer from his neighbors.

A correctional officer described his difficulty in not getting involved:

> I've got a couple of friends that own a bar and right after I started in corrections, they almost felt like I was a "rent-a-cop." If there was trouble in the bar, somebody would look

at me to go take care of it. I guess that bothered me. I figured I'm a customer. I do that at work, I don't do that here.

You may find yourself in a quandary as to whether to take action or not. Even though acquaintances may not actually expect you to take action, you often hear comments like: "Oh, oh, we've got to be careful. There's cops here."

Police and correctional officers are seldom introduced by name, only. It is usually, "Meet John Doe, the cop or guard," which immediately tells others: "This person is not a citizen. He or she is an officer. Be on your guard." This puts you in a position where you become a target for everyone who has ever had problems with any police or correctional officer:

There was one woman who was very hostile at me for being a cop because she doesn't like cops 'cause she got arrested once. So right away I had a problem there.

I could have been anything else, and no one would have thought of being my victim. But what other profession do you run into people who hate you because one of your profession did such and such to you?

At every gathering, it seems, someone has gotten a parking ticket they "didn't deserve," or knows someone who did, or has had some other unfavorable contact with police officers.

Correctional officers may not be socially involved in the same way as they were before becoming officers for fear of meeting former inmates:

I won't hang around with a lot of people that I used to. I used to be a bartender, and I used to know a lot of people that have real different kinds of life styles. I don't hang around with those people any longer. The possibility of me running into somebody from here, an inmate on the street in that kind of situation. I don't want to put myself in that kind of a situation.

Different Perceptions of Reality. Another barrier to social involvement is based on different perceptions of reality. This different view originates with a loss of innocence and is enhanced by fears of being socially unacceptable:

> It does create some distance between some friends. And it makes me real cautious with friends to let that guard down. So I talk about things in a cavalier way. You can talk to other police officers, and they understand completely. But your friends don't understand how you can feel so cold. It has caused me to not open up as much, and I am a little guarded in my off-hand comments. So there's a loss of spontaneity and some closeness when you don't share things with your friends.

Just as you fear self-disclosure, you may fear social non-acceptance. Because of your exposure to people and experiences resulting in a loss of innocence, you may have developed a different view from that of your friends that makes continuing friendships difficult. "I can feel alone in a room full of people because I just feel like I don't have anything in common with them. They don't see anything my way."

Fear of Being Inappropriate. You may feel uncomfortable in many social settings for fear of saying something inappropriate. "I feel I need to watch what I say, because my humor might not be understood or because it might sound callous."

You may also develop a protective, icy exterior which is inappropriate in most social settings. You are used to keeping an emotional isolation at work and cannot readily discard it in a social setting.

You were not born as an isolated individual who later gathered to form an isolated group: "I've become somewhat of a loner, and I wasn't before. I was high school class president, active in sports, on the paper, in the band, and all of the things a kid did. I think that actually over the years I've become isolated."

Another officer described his isolation as intentional:

> When I first became a sergeant, I was working the north side stations and I was young and aggressive and made some mistakes, and was very by-the-book and got the reputation of

being an asshole. And knew it, and it didn't bother me.
That was part of the job. I accepted that part of it.

One of the advantages was that once you obtained that
reputation, you don't ever have to be one. Nobody's going to do
something and hope that I'm going to cover it up.

The down side of that is, nobody is going to come to you
and confide in you that they need some help because they
don't trust you.

INEVITABLE ISOLATION

This isolation may be inevitable. Your tasks and image make
it very difficult to stay in the mainstream of the community.
Most officers feel a certain amount of alienation from the
community at large regardless of how they try to avoid it.

Isolation *is* a main tenant of the police group. As Blumberg and Niederhoffer (1976, p. 20) have stated:

> For far too long the police as an occupational group have
> been out of the mainstream of society. This is due to more
> than the fact that the individual police officers find comfort
> in mutual support. The police simply have not been part of
> the other institutional communities; rather they have been a
> beleaguered group, functioning in an almost self-segregated
> enclave that tended to nourish the often resentful style
> characteristics of other marginal groups in a society.

Correctional officers are isolated in many of the same ways
that Blumberg and Niederhoffer have identified for police
officers. You, too, find comfort in mutual support and in
many cases choose not to be part of mainstream society.

Finally, while you appear to socialize with others, that
socialization may not be "real." You may be giving little, if
any, of yourself. Consequently, you are still isolated:

> I wasn't close to anyone. I had good friends, but the friends
> I had were drinking friends or friends attending sporting
> events or parties or something like that. 'Cause good friends,
> I felt they were good, I still think they are, they're a lot of

fun, but there's no intimacy on my part. Nobody knew what I was about.

You may adjust and re-enter the mainstream of the community on some basis. You may even run for City Council, Mayor, or the state legislature, but you are still a cop or guard, with all the attached "baggage."

REFERENCE

Blumberg, A. S. and A. Niederhoffer. (1976). In Abraham S Blumberg and Arthur Niederhoffer. (Eds.). *The Ambivalent Force.* Springfield: Charles C. Thomas.

"I just love when I go to a party and get introduced as a cop."

This smile is painted on, too.

Chapter 10

CONSTRICTED AND INAPPROPRIATE AFFECT

You're required to be very cool and calculating when you dispense your emotions. You can't do it impulsively. I would have a calculated response to any occurrence.

Police and correctional officers frequently have difficulty expressing their emotions. You become accustomed to rigidly controlling any expression of emotional pain because such an expression could interfere with your work.

As a police officer you deal with tragedy daily. You are frequently exposed to people who are experiencing intense emotional pain. Often these people are in such pain they are not sure what to do next. So they look to you for guidance and decisions. But if you empathize too strongly with such people, you may be unable to perform your duties.

As a correctional officer, you can ill afford to appear weak or vulnerable because such an appearance could encourage challenge of your authority or attacks by the inmates.

NEED FOR CONTROL

While you must remain aloof enough to function, it is hard to not feel the pain of those you deal with. Still, you must remain *in charge*:

I have always felt that I am responsible, and I really have to
be in charge of the outcome. That went along with keeping
myself protected and keeping my guard up on my job. When
you get to something, you are expected to handle it. If the
cops can't fix it up, who else are they going to call?

An officer talking with a rape victim may find her pain is
expressed in every word she says. It is difficult to get the
information needed to perform official duties without hearing
that pain, even though you may desperately want to *not* hear
it. On *Dragnet*, Sgt. Joe Friday became famous for saying,
"Just the facts, Ma'am."   As one officer said: "That attitude
is basically just a shell they built up to protect themselves from
the realities of the job."

Correctional officers may find it difficult to connect with
inmates who have inflicted such pain. You may have difficulty
understanding how inmates could rape an elderly woman, beat
a child, or kill a wife. The reality is that these individuals not
only could commit the crimes as charged, they did.

Denial of Emotions. As you live more and more in the world
of perpetrators and victims, it becomes more and more
difficult to keep the pain from affecting you personally. To
remain unaffected by that pain, you must keep your emotions
under rigid control.

You may fear that if you once let your emotions out, you
will be unable to control the deluge. You may be afraid that
if you allow yourself to cry, you may be unable to control how
hard you cry, how often, and under what circumstances:

I store it away. It's bad, but I've been doing it for a number
of years, and I've done it even before I became an officer.
And I know it's bad, and I know that some day it's going to
all explode on me.

Even though you may intellectually understand the detri-
mental effects of such control, it is still part of your defenses:
"You build a wall, and no one gets in."

Denial of Pain. A by-product of this control is that you believe you must not acknowledge your *own* pain or that other's pain can affect you. This becomes a reason not to invest in relationships so as not to become vulnerable:

> It's taught me to rely on myself. Like I said, whether or not I can do it, it's taught me to believe that I can. And that probably had a lot to do with other people because I guess it would be like you become controlling of anybody you come into contact with.

This control can extend into other areas of your life. You cannot go home and subject your spouse to an outpouring of tears. Nor can you alternate between *feeling* in your personal life and *not feeling* in your professional life. This transition is difficult, if not impossible:

> It's hardened me. My wife tells me how much I've changed. I don't see it. Maybe I just won't accept it. You know how it hardens you then. And it does. It's got to harden you because if you were to be more like her [your wife], it would blow your mind away. You'd eat your gun.

Denial of Vulnerability. This difficulty stems from an inability to accurately express feelings to yourself or others and is a barrier to effective social interaction. You may tend to invest less of yourself in relationships because you don't want others to see your vulnerabilities or pain. It is crucial to hide those vulnerabilities:

> If you show a little weakness they'll eat ya up. Within a department or when you're dealing with the public, it's the same thing. If you show a little weakness, they will come down on ya, and you'll just never live it down. So you're required to be very cool and calculating when you dispense your emotions. You can't do it impulsively. You have to think, and you have to think about the proper emotion [to show].

This is one reason you may find it easier to be with those you are not close to. There is safety in a lack of commitment:

> I have a problem with a commitment and intimacy at the same spot. And I'm not willing to risk a lot of it. I don't want to risk the intimacy where I have the commitment. I can be much more intimate with someone I'm not committed to because the hell with them, what's the difference? I can tell them anything I want, and they can think what they want, and I don't ever have to hear it again.

Denial of Danger. You can also use control to deny the dangers of the job. It becomes an intellectual exercise that there is danger, but that danger is negated because you are "in control." It may be terrifying for anyone to realize just how little they can actually control risks. It becomes increasingly important for you not to acknowledge this lack of control because it would interfere with the job—which *is* to control:

> You have to be in control in this job, and that's not all bad. I think you have to know what you're doing, and you have to be able to have confidence when you go in somewhere that you're doing things right. If it's something that's potentially threatening, you have to know what you're doing. So I think it's good to have that confidence in yourself, but you can't disassociate from work to anything else.

Denial of Fear. Another area where control plays an important role is the expression of fear. It is not okay to be afraid. You can be angry. You can laugh. You can be cynical. But you cannot be afraid:

> The basement was dark. There were so many hallways, so many doorways, we never knew when he was going to jump out. He was a loon case, no doubt about it. He had just taken a cop's gun. He was crazy. . . . But we didn't talk a whole lot about whether it was just plain scary to do our job. It was not okay to be afraid.

SUBSTITUTES FOR AFFECT

This inability to display affect may force you to release occupational and relationship stress through other channels:

I suppose if you can't talk about them, then you deal with them sideways, and usually that comes out. And if it's not direct, the only valid feeling is anger. So let it come out, come out as anger or come out as jokes or cynicism.

Sideways may show itself physically or in emotions such as anger, so called "black humor" or other "acceptable" ways.

Physical Substitutes. A primary direction in which these repressed energies surface is physical: back pain, teeth grinding, hypertension, and heart attacks.

Because the police job involves a lot of riding in cars, some struggling with suspects, and an occasional fight for your life, it is often difficult to tell which physical pains are stress-related and which are a direct result of work-related physical incidents.

You may have difficulty sleeping after work and need to unwind. This unwinding can take the form of a few beers after work, isolation, mood changes, physical exercise, or just more difficulties to repress.

Anger and Laughter. It is acceptable to display some emotions, but these are limited to anger and laughter, both included in the "John Wayne" syndrome: "Men are not allowed to have those emotions—be strong and silent, but don't ever cry." You need to be strong and silent. It is all right to get angry or to laugh, but *never* to cry.

The range of emotions you permit yourself or your peers to display is severely limited. When you feel pain, sadness, or fear, an acceptable emotional display is anger: "The only emotion that you can show effectively is anger. That's acceptable. All others are weakness. So you live on anger, and you live on jokes. You adopt a black humor. That keeps you going."

Black Humor. Laughter becomes another substitute emotion. You may use "black (sick) humor" as a cover for other feelings. This is done because: "Black humor injects a little levity into really sad situations. It keeps you from crying."

As another officer said: "You saw something that really bothered you. You wouldn't say that it really bothered you and really affected you. You'd make some joke about it." Black humor is used in situations that call for tears. The laughter covers those tears:

> The black humor injects a little levity into really sad situations. It keeps you from crying or feeling sorry for someone. You get someone that's committed suicide with a shotgun, and you say, "Well, he got a bang out of that." And the ones that are hanging, "We told you to quit hanging around here," and things like that.
>
> Little jokes. "I wonder if we can sell this guy's shoes?" and "What size is the coat?" and "How big is the hole in it? We can have it mended . . ." and a few things like that. And so it's kind of a callous humor that you get.

As you become more callous, specific groups may become targets for black humor. It becomes easier to poke fun at members of a group's unusual mannerisms or traditions:

> If you're really angry with a specific group of people, you might start whenever you see groups of people like them. Then you would start making jokes about those people. If you're riding in the car with your partner picking out mannerisms of those people and embellishing on them and playing those out. A lot of it is just sort of passive-aggressive hostility coming out—using comedy as a way to dump whatever reasons you have for these hostile feelings that you have inside you.

Black humor is not limited to work situations. It becomes a coping mechanism that can extend into your day-to-day living:

> Nothing is sacred with that type of humor... It's a cover-up and everybody uses it. But it's very effective. I think when

you do something long enough, it becomes part of you, and that transmits back into your family.

An officer may come home from work to be greeted by his wife who is in tears. When the officer asks what's wrong and she replies that the baby fell off the couch, the officer may ask, "How high did she bounce?" This black humor covers the officer's concern, but may not be an appropriate response to his wife's concern.

As black humor becomes more and more ingrained, you may become unsure of yourself in social situations, afraid of what you might say and how it might be interpreted by others. Friends may not find the black humor amusing or appropriate. They may, instead, find it tasteless and disgusting: "I feel like I need to watch what I say because the humor might not be understood or might be callous."

Substitute Actions. Just as anger and laughter may substitute for deeper emotions, actions may also substitute for emotions. Emotions can be covered with sex, alcohol, work, or even violence:

You'd drink over it, you could have sex over it, you could party over it, you could buy toys, you could work a lot, rather than face our feelings. And I did most of these things rather than face my feelings.

Another officer said:

You can get together [with other police officers] in anger, you're close and you're real close when you're having fun or when you're drinking, but when you feel really sad, you go do that by yourself. That's a private thing that's done by yourself. You don't share that.

Some feelings and substitutes are acceptable; others are not. Police and correctional work is not conducive to intimacy. It frequently emphasizes the negative. It may be angry, violent, distrustful, and cynical: "There was booze and sex and violence and all that, but there wasn't much place for

intimacy." While you may not define intimacy, you probably
realize that your work is a lot of things other than intimate.
You don't know what intimacy is, only what it is *not*.

AN EMOTIONAL VOID—LACK OF AFFECT

After repressing your emotions long enough, you may have
serious doubts as to whether you even feel emotions: "By not
showing them [emotions], I think that eventually you get
where you don't even feel them either."

One officer experienced emotional difficulty after responding to a call where a child was killed by its mother: "I just
didn't know what to do [emotionally]. I knew something was
wrong, but I had no idea what. There was nothing there."

The emotional difficulties did not stem from an inability to
control the emotions, but rather from difficulty in *experiencing*
the emotions that you wanted and needed to feel. Even if you
stop *feeling* emotions, you may still display them:

> I would have a calculated response to any occurrence. If
> something happened, I would think, "Well, I think I will
> show a little happiness now." And I would be happy. And
> if something bad happened, I would think, "Well, I better
> show a little anger." So I made my point with anger. And
> if something really sad happened, I would do nothing. I
> would just eat it.

While the police and corrections occupations require
control of emotions, it is neither healthy, nor even possible, to
eliminate your emotional nature. It is a psychological axiom
(truth) that emotions need not be logical. How often have
you said something like, "I know it doesn't make sense, but
that's the way I feel."

Police work, being logical in nature, is *inconsistent* with
emotions. It involves logical "proofs" and "one-step-to-the-
next investigation." You are expected to translate the
emotional pain of others into logical proof. As you do this,
you also translate your own pain into logic. This

self-translation doesn't work, and you are left with something you no longer allow to be emotion, but have not made the impossible leap to logic.

You may ask yourself, no *insist*, that you not permit yourself to become involved emotionally.   You demand emotional sterility:

> I think we, ourselves, as the police community are probably the biggest culprits in that regard by expecting our fellow officers to be superhuman and exemplary and in everything they do, which is not possible. And when someone falls off this pedestal we've placed ourselves on, then everyone's very quick to point fingers, and I think it's a very high price that the policeman pays for doing a job.

"Everything's fine . . .   Why?"

They're here for each other.

Chapter 11

IMPORTANCE OF THE POLICE–CORRECTIONS FAMILY

Until you've sat and looked at your partner after you've told a child's parents that their child is dead–and neither of you can put into words what you feel or make any sense of what has happened–and you know that right now your partner is the only person in the world that can know what you've been through, you can't understand how important a partner can be.

Police work is not a science. It's a folk art that has been passed down from one generation of police officers to the next. To be a successful police officer, you *must* fit into the system. Most police officers do not leave the department because they don't like the work. They leave because they don't fit into the system. They are not "one of the group."

Neither can correctional officers function in a vacuum. They cannot work in their prison without the help and support of their fellow officers:

I believe that the people that I worked with would have done anything for me, and in times they have. They didn't even mind giving me money. If I needed booze, they gave booze. If I needed sex, they find somebody to take care of that for me.

THE OCCUPATIONAL CULTURE

Police and correctional officers form their own subculture, and that group is extremely important to individual officers. Your involvement, however, goes much deeper than that. Each police department and prison has its own "personality." Certain things are acceptable for officers of one department, but not another. Things that are "OK" in one prison may not be in another.

Not only do police and correctional officers form important groups, but the officers of each group form an incredibly tight-knit family. The police family determines the "personality" of the police department. Likewise, the correctional family determines the "personality" of the prison. It also significantly affects the lives of individual officers.

Informal Rules. Officers, as a group, informally determine what is acceptable behavior within legal limits. This group may also determine if it is permissible to act outside the scope of their legitimate authority and how. Most often, the group decides what types of laws or regulations are most prestigious to enforce and what activities are permissible in that enforcement. This group establishes the informal rules by which you operate.

If a department emphasizes traffic enforcement and you have 500-plus traffic citations, you will be well thought of by your peers. In a department that emphasizes felony arrests, however, the number of traffic citations you have may actually work against your prestige. In an institution that emphasizes rehabilitation, if you are rigid and see everything in black and white, you may not fit. Conversely, in an institution that prizes order, if you are more interested in inmates' individual problems, you may be negatively branded a "social worker."

INFLUENCE BEYOND THE JOB

The occupational family's influence goes well beyond the job and may extend into your personal life as well. The group determines acceptable stress reducers. Drinking after work, for example, may be an acceptable stress reducer, while playing handball is not. Anger and laughter are often the only accepted emotions, as noted in the previous chapter.

THE OCCUPATIONAL FAMILY

The police or corrections culture can become all-encompassing: "I got all this confidence in police officers. Then I just lost it all with the family. I never talked to them any more." Other officers have described how important the police "family" becomes: "It becomes easier to be involved with other officers because they not only don't ask for intimacy, they refuse to accept it."

Correctional officers also find that the occupational "family" becomes more and more important:

It's dangerous, so you'd be with the people you could trust. You spend a lot of time with them and share the same experiences. You want to be sure there's somebody there to back you up. In the early days it was a real dangerous place to work. I've been taken hostage. I've been stabbed, assaulted many, many times. The point is, the people that were with you, you knew you could count on and be there.

So you drank and you partied. You were with them all the time, so my family suffered. Like my wife said, she and my social life with my family suffered. I didn't do anything unless it was with the guys. So I think the penalty I paid was failed marriages and quality time with my children.

You may put your career first and your role as husband or wife, father or mother second. You may lose your family because the people you work with take their place, becoming a substitute family. You need no other family, especially a family you believe cannot understand what you feel or experience.

Your spouse may feel like an outsider and see the job as a "jealous lover" demanding more and more from you.

Like Talking to Yourself. As intimacy becomes more and more difficult, the "job-family" may become more and more important to you: "You feel captured by your own experience because the only people you can relate to is other officers. And yet relating to them is like talking to yourself because they can't relate to anybody else." Another officer said:

> I had finished my second divorce and was living alone. I don't think I was sober more than an hour a day, and that was toward the end of my sleep cycle. As soon as I got up, it didn't matter if I was working or not, I was drinking.
>
> I called a guy, a close friend, and told him everything that was going on. We sat in a bar and got just whacked. Well, what good did that do? Three days later I wasn't feeling any better. Nothing changed. They'll listen to you, but there's no constructive feedback or help.

Divorce. The job may become so all-consuming your spouse may give an ultimatum: "Me or the job." In looking at officers' exceptionally high divorce rate, the decision of many is apparent.

MINORITY GROUP STATUS

Another characteristic of the occupational family is its "minority group" status. You develop a sense of belonging to a minority group. You see yourself as isolated from the mainstream of society, but with power few others are granted legitimately, and often subjected to different treatment because of your group membership.

The occupational group power helps you assume this feeling of minority group status. Psychologist, Carl Jung (1933), has said in this regard:

> To think otherwise than our contemporaries think is some-how illegitimate and disturbing; it is even indecent, morbid or blasphemous, and therefore socially dangerous for the individual. He is stupidly swimming against the social current.

A Minority with Power. One notable difference between the police and correctional officers and other minority groups is that officers are a minority group with *physical power and legal authority.* You have been expressly empowered by the community to use physical force, if necessary, "to preserve law and order" for a community you may feel has isolated you.

Visibility. The stereotype is fostered by the uniform worn, distinguishing you from other members of society. Skolnik (1975, p.69) suggests:

> The policeman is a unique kind of user of the city streets. He develops an intimate knowledge of the places he works, a knowledge of his territory not matched by many of the people who live there. He knows it better than his own neighborhood, but he is not "at home" there. He does not know most of the people he sees or is called to assist, but everyone knows that he is a policeman.
>
> Every aspect of his appearance has been calculated to assure that there can be no mistake about his social identity. His uniform not only makes him visible to people who wish to find him, but limits his snooping directly in the lives of citizens; it also gives an unequivocal statement to everyone that the person intervening in their lives is not a private person, but a cop.

The separateness reinforces the tendency of police and correctional officers to close ranks. You have all the feelings and some of the responses that minority groups have when they are or feel isolated from society.

In dealing with other minority groups, police and correctional officers see a reflection of their own groups, however at odds the purposes of the groups may seem.

Secrecy. The officers' group cohesiveness is further enhanced by the secrecy under which they operate. You are seldom *immediately* accountable to anyone except yourself. Citizens are not really sure what you are *supposed* to be doing; hence, no one knows if you are doing what you should. Yet you are

expected to display a solidarity against the often misunderstanding public. And you do.

The secrecy surrounding officers is based on some very
legitimate and some not-so-legitimate reasons.

Reasons for Secrecy. The secrecy regarding officers and their
functions has evolved over the years to protect them from
criminals, to protect them from the people they deal with, and
to cover their human imperfections. Each underlying reason
for secrecy has been acknowledged by officers.

You need to protect yourself. Countless threats have been
made against police and correctional officers and their families
by people who have been arrested or who felt they have been
dealt with unfairly.

In most instances the threats are just that, simply threats
made in heated moments. But in some cases attempts *are*
made to carry out the threats, some successfully, some not.
You are never sure which category the current threat falls
into.

Statistics on threats made against police and correctional
officers are difficult to accurately compile. Usually the threats
are either simply included in an arrest report under another
heading or are not written down at all. Also police and
corrections machismo not only prohibits you from making an
issue of threats, but has influenced the courts to feel such
threats are part of the job.

The second reason for secrecy is that officers often feel a
need to protect themselves from those they serve. Even
though you may not realize or acknowledge it, you need time
away from other people's emotional pain so you have time to
heal. You need time to "recharge your battery"—to maintain
whatever psychological equilibrium you can muster. Correctional officers need to get away from the inmates to remember
that the world really can be a "good" place.

The third reason underlying secrecy is the need to cover
officers' human imperfections. It is difficult for anyone to
always live up to and perform as citizens expect of police and
correctional officers. You are in the position of never being

able to make a mistake. Therefore, secrecy evolved to conceal any mistakes from the public.

What the public fails to realize, according to Blumberg (1975, p.21), is that: "When one is responsible for everything one is also vulnerable for the inevitable mistakes in carrying out the impossible."

This code of secrecy also tightens and further isolates officers as a group from society (Westley, 1976, p.161):

> Among the latent functions of the secrecy code one of the most important seems to be that it makes the individual policeman [or policewoman] identify with other policemen [or policewomen], and distinguish himself [or herself] from non-police officers. Thus it functions as a social bond among the police, by giving them something in common.

THE STEREOTYPE VS. REALITY

Officers form strong groups to defend themselves against public misunderstandings. The public finds in a stereotypical police or correctional officer a machismo they may not find in themselves.

TV Cops and Guards. Citizens are also bombarded with cop shows on television. They determine how police should behave by watching shows like *Hill Street Blues, T.J. Hooker,* and *Hunter.* Citizens come to expect their police to act the same way.

A citizen who sees television cops always getting the criminals (within one-half hour and between commercials) will wonder why *his* police can't even find out who broke his car window and stole his cassette player.

Citizens also see on television the old-time stereotype of the big Irish buffoon cop. This old-time beat cop steals an apple now and then from the corner fruit stand. While he may have the best intentions in the world, he "couldn't find a bass fiddle in a phone booth." This is the typical "Officer

O'Malley" depicted in cartoons or the old television series *Car 54, Where Are You?*

Television cops always seem to know the good guys from the bad guys and never have any trouble with the good guys. They are always there when someone needs help. Citizens can't understand the apparent ineptness of their real-life police compared to what they see daily on television.

They may see "new" laboratory techniques that haven't been invented yet, or interview techniques forbidden by the Constitution, and wonder why their officers don't use these "great investigative aids." These misconceptions tend to solidify the police group.

Many people have never met a prison guard. They learn what they are like from television and the movies. They have seen guards from *The Bridge on the River Kwai* to *Lock Up*. In *none* of these movies have the correctional officers been portrayed as real people. In those rare instances where a correctional officer is portrayed as human, he is also portrayed as an outcast, isolated from his peers.

Media Coverage. Citizens see the television and newspaper coverage of police and correctional officers' trials across the country. The officers and citizens are both exploited because of one-way news. An article describing how a police officer pulled an injured man from a burning car or a correctional officer who saved an inmate's life with CPR gets one small paragraph hidden in the middle of the paper. Yet any police or prison scandal is headlines, read by many more people.

People see the negative side of cops and guards just like cops and guards see the negative side of life. Citizens come to expect that cops and guards are "crooked," and the image of officers throughout the country is tarnished.

STRENGTHENING THE OCCUPATIONAL FAMILY

Having to enforce laws and regulations not everyone agrees with and the danger often associated with such enforcement are additional factors isolating officers and, consequently, strengthening the police "family." Skolnick (1976, p.91) says:

> The element of authority reinforces the element of danger in isolating the policeman. Typically, the policeman is required to enforce laws representing the puritanical morality, such as those regulating the flow of public activity, such as traffic laws. In these situations the policeman directs the citizenry, whose typical response denies recognition of his authority and stresses his obligation to respond to danger.
>
> The kind of man who responds well to danger, however, does not normally subscribe to codes of puritanical morality. As a result, the policeman is unusually liable to the charge of hypocrisy. That the whole civilian world is an audience for the policeman, further promotes police isolation and, in consequence, solidarity.

You are forced to rely heavily on your occupational group for acceptance. You are unlikely to look for acceptance from within the group you must regulate, that is, the citizens or inmates. You are so often in an adversarial role with those groups that it makes their approval meaningless or unattainable. You may tend to associate more and more often with other officers because they think like you:

> It becomes easier to be with other police officers because they have that basic understanding. They can see some of the things inside you.
>
> Some of the terminology is crude too. When I started, I didn't want to get into any words like *"scumbags"* and *"scrotes"* and all the other words, but it becomes a definition that you are aware of and your fellow officers are aware of. I really don't know if you could use other terms, it so aptly describes these people.

Group power tends to isolate you from society's mainstream because of the group's importance to individual members. As Skolnick (1976, p.1) puts it:

> The whole civilian world watches the policeman. As a result, he tends to be limited to the company of other policemen for

whom his police identity is not a stimulus to carping norma-
tive criticism.

You may feel somewhat secure in your occupational group
because there is no conflict between the social identity and
occupational identity. The National Advisory Commission on
Criminal Justice Standards and Goals (1973, p.35) said:

> Like everyone else, an officer needs self-respect. When he
> finds that his contacts with the public are frequently antago-
> nistic, and that some people slight his role, he may begin to
> feel alienated. This feeling of isolation often leads to
> development of a police subculture to which officers turn for
> comfort and respect.

Self-Image.   The group's power over you may be more
complete than most other groups over their members. One
thing that gives this group so much power is the attraction it
holds for its members. This attraction is not so much one of
desire as it is one of need.

Every officer needs the reflective self-image that can be
obtained from only his or her group. You need the acceptance and comradeship found within the group. You need the
group to help relieve the stress of the job. Finally, you need
the group because of the sanctions it can impose on officers
who do not accept it.

The self-image you need can be found consistently only
within your occupational group. For example, after work, your
group may get together to stabilize the self-images that have
been partially shattered by the day's contact with the public.
This often takes the form of an after-shift party at a special
bar or some other location. Maynard (p.14) states that these
parties after work serve as a relaxant and a stress reducer.

Support. Officers become so important to each other that
they serve as an almost exclusive source of support. They
become brothers, sisters, and perhaps even fathers and mothers.

Yet this "family" has its problems. The dictates are
exclusive, and the group's importance is paramount. To be

disowned by this family is disastrous. It can mean that you are labeled a "hot dog" or "coward" by other officers. They choose not to work with you, or provide help when you really need it.

These families offer excitement and challenge that your family at home cannot. It becomes easier and easier to spend more and more time with that group. Not only does this group offer excitement and challenge, but fellow officers determine who succeeds within the system, and so this family can become *everything* to you.

"I'm with you partner . . . . Why go home at eleven when the old lady's sleeping already."

REFERENCES

Blumberg, A. S. and A. Niederhoffer. (1976). In *The Ambivalent Force*. A. S. Blumberg and Arthur Niederhoffer. (Eds.). Springfield: Charles C. Thomas.

Jung, C. G. (1933). *Modern Man in Search of a Soul.* New York: Harcourt Brace Jovanovich.

Maynard, P.E. "Police Families, Families at Risk." (unpublished paper), p.14.

National Advisory Commission on Criminal Justice Standards and Goals. *Police.* (1973). Washington, D.C.: U.S. Government Printing Office. p.35.

Skolnick, J. H. (1976). *The Ambivalent Force.* A. S. Blumberg and Arthur Niederhoffer. (Eds.). Springfield: Charles C. Thomas.

Skolnick, J. H. (1975). *Police in America.* J. H. Skolnick and Thomas D. Gray. (Eds.). Massachusetts: Educational Associates. p.69.

Westly, W. A. (1976). *The Ambivalent Force.* A. S. Blumberg, and Arthur Niederhoffer. (Eds.). Springfield: Charles C. Thomas.

PART III

IMPLICATIONS

Part III begins by describing the personal effects of stress as you change, experience frustrations, develop coping mechanisms, and otherwise deal with the demanding schedule of police and corrections work (Chapter 12).

Implications for your family, including effects on your children, your homelife, and your spouse are explained in Chapter 13.

Many activities associated with the administration, are *perceived* as unfair and stressful by police and corrections officers. The administration may also be viewed as an adversary because of real or perceived insensitivity or lack of support (Chapter 14).

For trainers and supervisors of police and correctional personnel, knowledge of how stress affects officers is critical. It contributes to knowing what changes to expect, when and how to train, and how to effectively transform civilians into officers. The role of peer counseling and day-to-day supervision in reducing stress and its effects is also vital (Chapter 15).

Trained professionals, such as chaplains and counselors and clinicians who work with officers must be cognizant of the stress officers face and the programs available to help them deal with these stresses. Only then are they in a position to help officers who are "on the brink," those who are suffering from post-traumatic stress disorder or those who have been severely victimized. The support and understanding of peers and family members is also critically discussed. (Chapter 16).

"Where do I go from here?"

Chapter 12

MEANINGS FOR INDIVIDUAL OFFICERS

It changes you. I find that I've become even more conservative. Politically when I started I think I was pretty liberal, saying let's give the underdog a chance and let's do this and let's do that. You see that a lot of that doesn't work, and you become more conservative. Everyone's a little too liberal for me.

The "prices" discussed in Part II are *real*. They affect each police and correctional officer to some extent—some more than others. This chapter focuses on what all this can mean to you personally.

The single most important thing for officers is *change*. Everything changes. You are no longer the naive individual you once were. Your perceptions, outlook, goals, ambitions, and friendships change because of your occupational choice:

I guess my perception of being a police officer at that time, of course, was to go out and end crime in the city, lock up all the criminals in the city and all that. I found within about a month later that that obviously wasn't reality at all. I wasn't going to lock up all the criminals because once I got off my eight-hour shift, I mean they were still out there going strong.

CHANGE

Nothing is as it was before. You work when others are sleeping, do things no one else wants to do, and laugh at jokes

155

no one else thinks are funny. Your world turns upside down compared to what it was.

You realize you have changed since becoming a cop or guard and also realize you had no control over the direction or extent of the change: "Most of the people that come into this type of work are real high quality human beings, not necessarily high education or anything like that, but just good human beings. And then they get messed up." Another officer described his process of change like this:

> I think a price that we all go through is psychological change. I think everybody's been through that from a shy young kid that comes on the police force through that fifth year where you're a super tough, aggressive cop and can whip anybody in the world. I think your family suffers through your growing up through that era. Then you get the tapering realization that you're human like everybody else.

A third officer said:

> I always thought about when I first came on it was kind of neat. I went to the oral interview, and they asked me, "What makes you think you would be a good police officer?" I said that it was because I didn't have a temper, I was easy to get along with people, and there would be no problems.
>
> Then they said, "Well, why do you think you wouldn't be a good cop?" And I said maybe because I would be too easy. I'd be gullible or whatever.
>
> I think it's just not that way anymore. I don't believe anybody. I don't believe anything. When I came on, I don't believe I had any prejudices or I don't ever remember having a temper or anything like that. Now, like I say, I just don't believe anybody, distrustful of people.

While you may be initially "innocent," such innocence is soon lost. You may have entered police or correctional work without any idea of what the job entails:

> I knew there was crime, I knew there were people out there that weren't nice, but no one could tell me then about man's inhumanity to man. I didn't believe that this stuff could go on, that

people could do the things that they do. Ah, then I see it, even now, even though I see it, I don't believe some of it. I mean it happens. I think I was living under a rock.

FRUSTRATION

You probably became an officer to "help people," but often find your efforts thwarted: "The hardest thing for me to realize was that not everyone who needed help wanted it."

You can do little things on the side to make people feel better, and once in a while you get a case you can really work up and really get something good out of it. But for the most part, as I found out the hard way, cops aren't the ones that are going to fix the system. It has gotta be somebody else.

The transition from caring to frustration is extremely stressful:

And when you care a lot and constantly get frustrated because things don't change, I mean I can go out in the street tomorrow and people would still be shooting each other up on the north side, and drunks would still be laying under the bridges. Nothing changes. You just walk away from it, and it goes on like you've made absolutely no impact.

You may become hardened and callous, not out of choice, but simply to survive:

I've really changed. It's the job has changed me in the fact that I think I've gotten a little more, I know this is almost going to sound kind of contradictory of what I just said, but kind of more callous towards some people as far as you always look at the 10 percent of the assholes that commit the crime and you think that the other 90 percent are just as goofy as they are.

Correctional officers can become frustrated by rules and regulations that get in the way and by bureaucratic philosophies made by those who don't need to enforce them.

COPING MECHANISMS

To cope with the changes you experience, you learn new skills. You learn to isolate yourself from those you work with and to use "black humor" to lighten the load of other people's pain. But when black humor fails, you may turn to other methods to lessen the pain—alcohol, drugs, or even suicide. In effect, you may become alone in a world filled with other people's pain. You have no one you feel comfortable talking to about these matters and can't admit you feel alone. You believe no one understands because no one sees the world as you do:

> I got real uncomfortable many times going and talking to my health program about hemorrhoids or anything else. I just wasn't comfortable with that. I sure as hell wasn't going to go out there and talk to them about how I hurt inside and how I wanted to blow my brains out.

ISOLATION

The first new coping skill you learn is to isolate. You learn to isolate yourself from *victims,* to give yourself time away from their pain. In fact, you may learn this skill too well. You may isolate yourself not only from victims, but from your friends, families, and even your own feelings.

You learn to isolate from your *friends* because you find little in common with them anymore.

> When I talk about the frustration about why I don't feel any sympathy when certain people get done in, or the frustration with the court systems, or the frustrations of dealing with drunks, and the social programs that never seem to work and all the money that's put into it, most of my friends just don't understand what I'm talking about.

You isolate from *family* because they don't understand and you don't want them to. You don't want to expose those you love to your daily world:

I started to be different, and my wife stayed basically the same. And all of a sudden I couldn't really go to her and say this is what's happening, 'cause if I wanted to dump this stuff on her, she didn't know where to go with it. If I dumped some heavy stuff on her that wasn't good, then she probably didn't know how to talk about it or relate to it anyway.

Sometimes even when you are home, it is only physically. You may need time alone to get rid of the residual pain of others—often the only legacy from a day's work. Ultimately, you may isolate from your family with divorce. You also learn how important other officers are, as seen in Chapter 11.

An emptiness may pervade your world. You no longer have old friends, family, or even the self you were. Often, those with whom you work are used, however inappropriately, to fill this void.

IMPORTANCE OF THE JOB

The police or corrections job, culture, and "family" is decidedly important. Individuals continue to be officers, subjecting themselves to the consequences, for different reasons:

I say Bullshit. This job was me. This job was my life, and I care about this job. I cared too much. I don't know, lived it [life] eight hours at a time. Didn't give a damn about a whole lot. Didn't see any future in anything.

This officer found his job so important that it was all that kept him alive.

WORK SCHEDULE

Another aspect of the work that affects and changes most officers is the varied work schedule. Whether you rotate shifts or start on nights and move to the day shift as seniority increases, the schedule is a change.

Your work schedule varies, often changing a biological rotation from day hours to night hours being the waking hours. This change is dramatic: "It's the hours. It's just an entirely different type of life style."

The work schedule may become a problem, especially as you get older, because you probably do not function well in this physiological rotation. You may become physically ill, tired, irritable, and withdrawn: "I think just the fact that you're always changing your schedule is hard physically. It's hard socially on you, and it's hard mentally on you, too."

Rotating shifts are a real problem for many officers:

I think rotating shifts are real bad for the body. You just get used to this one shift, and boom—we rotate every month, so you're on the next shift. And I think when you're on the night shift, then a lot of times when I'm off, I'll end up going to bed early and get up early the next day. But then I go in that night, and then I'm up for the whole day. That's bad on your body.

One officer described difficulties with the hours like this:

Probably my main hang up about physical problems would be those with changing shifts. You can't eat right. You can't sleep right. Your social life is screwed up. Your family life is screwed up. And that, of course, kind of leads into the psychological part of it, which is the big price we pay.

Physical problems, however, may be experienced from more than just the hours:

I think that because you're on patrol that you tend to eat more junk food and everything. It's no good eating burgers all the time. So I don't eat like I would like to.

I don't get that regular exercise that I would like to. And I don't get the sleeping patterns that give you a sense of well being.

You may notice a decline in health. This is partially due to the hours, but also due to the job. You may work afternoons or evenings, especially if you are a younger officer. Even when you have more "whiskers" on the department and can work day shifts, the years of working nights have established a pattern of social relationships. The work hours cause problems because they tend to isolate you from friends:

> I think in police work you separate yourself from a lot of the members and functions of the community just because of the hours you work. So when you do end up getting day shift hours, I still haven't gotten the swing of things with other people and the neighbors and things like that.

Not only do the work hours isolate you from friends, they cam cause problems in relationships in general:

> The work hours takes its toll. A lot of people have holidays and weekends off, and they do things. I would, but I don't have those hours off.

Relationships also change because many civilians tend to stereotype police and correctional officers. One officer described an interaction with a new neighbor after the neighbor discovered he lived next door to a cop:

> "You don't look like a policeman." And I asked him, I said, "What does a policeman look like?" He said, "I don't know." and then drove off. But see, he had this image of me being in this uniform twenty-four hours a day. He wasn't used to seeing people... He didn't realize policeman got off and did their yard work and everything.

SUMMARY

No aspect of your life is unaffected by the job. You *must* change to survive. Your emotions are battered almost constantly with other people's problems. Your social relationships change. Your family life is affected. Even your physiology may become upset. Given the breadth and depth of these changes, stress is inevitable. It is also manageable (See Chapters 17 and 18).

A retired police officer with 25 years on the job (Parry, 1989, p.1A) said: "You have to lose your feelings in order to see and do the things you have to do to be a good police officer." This officer's story has a positive ending. After he retired, he *worked* at being more positive and upbeat.

He took a job as a guard at a hospital and became friends with Eric, a six-year-old patient with a rare form of leukemia. This little boy wanted to be a cop when he grew up. Knowing Eric wouldn't live that long, the officer had a police uniform made in Eric's size and packed it up along with a pair of handcuffs and a plastic gun. It didn't seem like enough, so he tucked in his gold sergeant's badge. Although it was hard to part with, the badge made his gift extra special.

Eric was enthralled with the gift. He wore the uniform and badge constantly, sometimes even sleeping with them on. Through his relationship with this young boy, the officer began to smile more, laugh more, and was even able to cry: "When Eric made me cry, he made me feel human again. I hadn't cried in 40 years."

REFERENCES

Parry, K. (1989). "Former Policeman Gives Boy His Old Badge and Gets Back His Feelings." *Star Tribune*. December, 1, 1989. p. 1A, 21A.

Roll call - THEN

Roll call - NOW

Be careful.

Chapter 13

MEANINGS FOR OFFICERS' FAMILIES

When I first came on the department, I think I got big badge syndrome–Joe Cop. And I think my family suffered from that. The job never suffered. I was always a policeman first, a husband and father second. I remember when I went to rookie school, a cop told me, told the whole school, that "broads and booze" are going to interfere in your life, and I told myself, "Bullshit."

But it was true. It did. It interfered with my life, but not my job. I wanted to be a cop. To me a cop was about the most important thing there was. I wanted to go and catch the bad guy. I wanted to wear the uniform, and because of that my family suffered.

The families of police and correctional officers are just as affected by this occupational choice as the officers themselves.

EFFECTS ON CHILDREN

Officer's children are not just anybody's kids. They are "cop's kids" or "guard's kids." This is, in some ways, like being the minister's son or daughter. The children are lumped together by an indifferent, uninformed public. Correctional officers' children may also be called "cop's kids."

Problems With Peers. Your children may be held to unreasonable standards by their peers, and when they get into trouble as *all* children do at some time, it is atrocious. They should know better—they're cop's kids.

On the other hand, your children may be taunted by peers, dared to do something to prove they are not "narcs" just because their father or mother is a police or correctional officer.

If other kids are caught in the midst of some misdeed, your children are likely to be blamed for "telling." Other children seem to *believe* that officers' children will tell their parents, whether they did or not. This perception can spread rapidly throughout neighborhoods and schools. Soon everyone "knows" that officers' children are not to be trusted. It becomes difficult for them to develop close friendships due to the almost automatic suspicion they must overcome.

One officer's nineteen-year-old daughter, when asked for an example of the effect of being an officer's child said:

Oh, God, there are thousands. Whenever my friends have parties, you know, with beer and stuff, I usually don't get invited. They are afraid that I'll tell my father.

Another thing is that guys don't like to ask me out because they're afraid of my dad. They're afraid that he'll interrogate them when they come over to the house.

One officer described the situation at her home when she said:

What's at home is two teenagers and a second grader. And the oldest is a girl. She's going to be seventeen. She's "in love" with a different boy every other day. And so there's a lot of, "Oh, Mom, I met this new boy," and right away it's, "What's his name? Where does he live? What do his parents do? What's his date of birth?" This type of thing.

And I wouldn't have done that before. Naturally, I would have been concerned for my kids or what my daughter thinks. But now I run records on all these people that she knows.

Another officer described some problems his son was having:

My oldest son used to have to fight because of what his dad did for a living. I mean, his dad's a policeman. Well, if his dad's a carpenter, how come he don't have to fight because his dad's a carpenter?

Lack of Parental Trust.   Your children also suffer the suspicion of a father or mother who is not only trained to trust no one, but is very practiced at not trusting. You learn every day *not* to trust because every day people lie in order to manipulate you.

When talking with your children, you may also be much less likely to believe what they say than other parents: "I think the same things were true with my son, who's eighteen. He's had to *prove* his innocence rather than me accepting it."

The seesaw of being distrustful part of the time and trusting at other times is a difficult transition to make from work to home, and since survival is most important, you are not trusting.

This is a double-edged sword because your children also learn not to trust from role models they admire. One young woman described it as "a feeling you get," and said that she "learned not to trust others" from her officer father: "You never know if people are telling the truth."

Lack of Parental Affection. Another problem may be lack of feelings or display of inappropriate emotions. Since you may be most comfortable expressing emotions as either anger or laughter, often little room remains to display the love and tenderness looked for in family settings.

The quiet warmth of a hug may be something children of cops and guards less often experience from their parents. It is difficult to be insulated from other people's pain at work and then be tender, caring, empathetic, and compassionate at home. Until you learn to appropriately deal with affect at work, you must remain insulated—from everyone.

Parents' Special Knowledge. Police and correctional officers know more about the community, crime, and the sordid side of life in general than others and, consequently, respond differently when their children want to go to "so and so's house," or to this shopping mall, or to that roller rink. You know what has happened at these places, and even though they may have been isolated incidents, you do not want your children exposed to or involved in trouble:

> I know things that are going to keep me from being willing to take certain risks. I have a daughter, and she's always hated what I know because she wants to take a bus downtown, and I won't let her get off a bus on some streets downtown, and it's like, "Sometimes I hate that you know what goes on down there, because it's not fair. Other kids' moms don't know, and they let them go." And I said, "Yeah, but I know."

Another officer said: "I really don't trust people for my own safety and even my loved ones' physical safety because people can act irrational at any moment and could harm me so . . ." He went on to describe things he did not allow his wife and children to do because of possible consequences.

Not only do you know where the most crime is, you often tend to generalize:

> When my kids want to go to skateland or to the shopping mall, there were quite a few years when I just wouldn't let them go at all because those places were hotbeds for perverts and people selling dope to kids.

Another officer said:

> I became very protective of my family. When I thought of the criminal before I started here [a prison], it was the bank robber, the occasional murderer, and you really didn't think about child molestation and rape, some really gut wrenching things that really hit you personally, especially if you're a father. You see these things happening all over and think they could easily happen to my family or my spouse, you become very protective.

Work Schedules.   Officers work a great variety of hours. You may work mornings, afternoons, nights, or a mixture of the three shifts in any given week. As a result, your family suffers because you often miss birthday parties, school plays, and your children's sporting events. The children grow up without you.

Homelife. Families of police and correctional officers often do many things alone because of the work schedule. As you become more and more involved with the police or prison life, more and more problems may arise at home:

> I got married when I first became a policeman. So the fact that I was a policeman was not a surprise to my wife. But ultimately I think that the time element and rotating shifts caused problems. I think she may have felt somewhat threatened as if the job was almost another lover. She probably felt that she was on the outside looking in to some extent. I did devote a lot of time to my job, and not to her like maybe she wanted.

Time and Energy Drain. You want to do a "good job," but trying to do a job that can never be finished leads to complications. Your self-esteem becomes tied into how well you do your job: "I felt if I put in a lot of time and a lot of dedicated hard work, I would be successful as a policeman."

Police and correctional officers deal with many complex human problems. As such, you tend to devote an inordinate amount of time and energy to your work. This leaves less for your family, and that portion of your life may suffer.

Time spent at work and with other officers may begin to replace time with family:

> I was married and had one son and one that was going to be born just after I came on. And I always did things with the family and with my parents. Then I came on this job, and it became my whole life. It became my family–became everything.

Another officer described it this way:

> So I moved away from my family. I ended up getting a divorce. I know that there are a lot of reasons for my divorce, but I think if I had never become a policeman I never would have gotten divorced. I may not have had the perfect marriage or been totally happy in it, but I know I never would have gotten

divorced because it wouldn't even come up. We were that type of a family that we stuck together thick and thin.

Bringing the Job Home. To leave the job at work is difficult, if not impossible. The situations you deal with can be so life impacting they leave painful memories, even if the pain was originally someone else's. To separate work and home becomes difficult:

> I always try to guard against bringing the job home with me. And my wife was a part of this system. She knew a lot about what was going on in the department. So we never really discussed police work at home.
>
> For the most part I tried to leave a lot of the garbage that went on at the station. I might talk to her about something, if I saw something really gruesome, I might tell her about it. But not in real descriptive terms or something that would really be how I was feeling. I was just telling her about the incident. That sort of relieved some of the pressure, but I always tried to keep it separate. I never brought it home.

Attempts to Relieve Stress. As you try different ways to relieve occupational stress, you may turn to alcohol at some point:

> At roll call a certain car was assigned to go get the beer, and we'd have our garage parties after work. That was our way of letting it off. And you were ruining your health. You were ruining your home life. You got home about the time the sun was coming up, and you're bombed out of your tree. The kids were going to school, and in the door you'd come.
>
> That's what made me stop drinking. I'd come home one morning just bombed, and I couldn't get in the door. And all of a sudden the door opened and I fell flat on my face. I looked up and saw my oldest boy.

Another way to deal with the effects of the job is to take time alone to recharge your battery: "When I'm involved with something like that, I usually get really exhausted, and I try to go home, and I let them know that I've had a bad day, that I'm really tired and need to spend some time alone."

LACK OF COMMUNICATION WITH SPOUSES

As you run on overload more and more, you need to withdraw more and more to relax and get rid of the effects of the job. As you become more withdrawn, communications become more strained with your spouse. Difficulty in communicating can lead to a loss of intimacy in the relationship:

> If I am off duty I would just as soon sit at home and watch the movies, usually movies about cops or Rambo. It is just something like that. Over the years it has become a real problem because my wife is more in touch with what isn't right with our relationship. A lot of that is my own distance from it.
>
> The job has made me that way in that I have never been able to explain to her what it is that I feel when I get home. A lot of times I don't even bother.
>
> Last night was a good example. Well the night before last we had that homicide. It was another in a string of serial killings. It was the third one we have had now, and the guy was a couple of weeks old, and it was really a "gagger." It was very vulgar. And I got home, and I tried to explain it, and I just couldn't paint a picture like I had seen it. It wasn't anything like I had seen or experienced. I just stopped talking about it. It just seemed dumb or pointless to try and do that.

This officer went on to say, however: "One of the things that I discovered about myself is that I would really like to be intimate with my wife, but don't know how."

As you progress through your career, your communication patterns are likely to change: "When we first started going together, I would tell her everything, I mean just everything. We would sit down and talk about it for a couple of hours. And now it just doesn't mix at all."

Another officer said:

> But I've noticed, yeah, that over the last couple of years, and that's something that I think has been a big change for me since I came on. Like I say, I did enjoy coming home and telling her this happened—I did this, I did that. Now I don't even want to tell her anything.

Your spouse probably wants to listen, to help relieve your stress. But you may not feel your spouse will understand:

> Like my wife says to me, "You can talk to me, I understand."
> "No, you don't. You're not out there. You don't understand. You just don't."
>
> A wife is somebody that you can come home to and open up to and bitch to and let it out, but they don't understand. They don't understand what it's like. They don't see it.... Another policeman will understand what you're talking about, but he's not going to sympathize with you because he's got the same problems.

Extra-Marital Involvements. Difficulty in communicating with your spouse and using alcohol as a stress reducer can lead to extra-marital involvements: "I'd go over to the saloon and get stiff, probably get a little party time. Sometimes I'd run and see my friend. I'd go and see her and spend some time with her. And with her it was okay to be sad." But for this officer, it was not "okay to be sad" with his wife.

Male officers describe involvements with other women in several different ways. Some just go talk with other women. Some develop alternate relationships. And some have affairs.

For one officer, other women were people who he could talk with when things were bad. He felt he didn't want to take the pain he was feeling home to his wife, so he would talk with other women about that pain:

> I think by talking to someone else about that problem, because they never dealt with that, they take a deeper feeling. They say, "My God, is that really true? How do you handle that?" So I think I can relate to someone different, to an acquaintance, better than I can my wife because you just don't want to take that stuff home.

As you become more unable to share true feelings and to relate what happens at work with your spouse, you need to do something with the stored emotional turmoil: "Because I didn't want to take it home, on different situations like that where you had no place to turn, you just kept it within yourself and felt isolated. In two or three days I'd forget it."

One officer summed up the problems with alcohol and other women when he said:

> I think that probably one of the biggest prices I paid was divorce. I think it was directly related to being a cop in that it was ah, the shit I got involved in–the drinking, the chasing women, was all afforded me because of the police department. I got a lot of free booze, got this groupie girlfriend, and I think that my family life has really suffered from me being a cop. Too many temptations.

Fear of Danger. Police and correctional work is also stressful on marriages because spouses do not really understand what the job is like. While you are denying the danger, your spouse is probably denying the safety.

One officer reported that after he was involved in a shooting, his wife could not understand. She wanted him to call her every hour from work to let her know he was all right, even though it might be in the middle of the night. Because of the shooting, his relationship suffered significantly:

> At the time my wife, every single time before I would leave for work, would beg me not to go to work, or to get a different job. She'd say: "If it happened once, it can happen again. And everybody said you were nothing but lucky to still be here today. If it wouldn't have been for that vest, you'd be dead." It's not because of the way I handled myself that I'm here today. It's strictly luck. So on that end she wanted me not to go to work.

Fear of Death. It can become extremely difficult for a spouse in such a situation to work toward a healthy, productive relationship. As you move toward intimacy, your spouse realizes that you may die tomorrow. Consequently, the move is away from intimacy to prepare for that eventuality.

Your spouse may experience *anticipatory grief* and begin, even though not necessarily consciously, to rehearse for your death. Moving further and further away helps assure that when the inevitable occurs, the pain is lessened.

Our culture has identified stereotypical police officers constantly living in danger and frequently dying in the line of duty. Deaths of actual police officers are extremely public, surrounded with much pomp and ceremony and attracting wide media coverage.

Officers' spouses are flooded with stories (both real and fictional) of officers' deaths. While the fear is generated culturally, it becomes much more personal looked at through the eyes of these officers' husbands and wives. As this potential for loss becomes more personalized, it becomes much more powerful as a potential reality:

> It got to the point where every time I went to work, my wife would cry. I didn't know where to turn. All I know is police work, and she can't understand. It is destroying my marriage, and I don't know what to do about it.

SUMMARY

Police and correctional officers must run a gauntlet to maintain healthy family relationships. It is difficult because of the great potential for withdrawal, separation, and divorce. Yet healthy relationships are *not* impossible:

> I really feel stupid for devoting so much of my energy and time into the job, where, in fact, it didn't make any difference. I find, now at least, I give them their time. I give them their quality time. It doesn't affect anything else I do. I can do it with less enthusiasm and still do a good job, at least I think it is.
>
> So now I don't have to take away from my family or my kids. I can take a day off and leave this job when there's something that probably should be done, where I couldn't do that before.

"Why go home and talk with the wife . . . ?   All she cares about are the bills."

Should a prison look like a country club?

Chapter 14

ADMINISTRATIVE MEANINGS

Work--work was the thing that kept me alive 'cause I really liked my job, and I had a great deal of pride in doing a good job on the street. I also had a great deal of pride in taking care of my family responsibilities as far as money was concerned, and the job gave me that.

It may seem that all too often the administration has little or no understanding of the plight of officers on the street or in the cell block. Some administrators are too far removed from the ranks to remember what the work is really like. It is normal to forget the pain of dealing with others' traumas, the frustration of not being able to help someone who really needs and wants it, and the unpleasantness of a drunk who throws up all over your clean uniform. It is easy to forget what it feels like to be surrounded by a dozen threatening inmates.

FEELING OF INADEQUATE SUPPORT

You are out there living with those issues *and* you may feel you are living with them alone. You may feel there is inadequate administrative support for your work. Not only might you feel hampered by the court system and public misunderstanding and criticism, but you may also *perceive* the administration to be even more hampering.

Dichotomy may be seen when the administration does not support officers' actions. You may feel that when your actions are criticized, your administration does not support the decisions you made on the street. This lack of support may lead to fear of getting involved in all but the most required actions:

> And now, you can't get anybody. You listen to the radio, and nobody backs anybody up now. They're afraid to do anything, mainly because of the chief. The chief said he's going to hang somebody, and he's out to do it. And it makes a cop scared to even go and try to work.
>
> I've had more and more uniformed coppers come up and tell me how lucky I am that I'm working where I am, that I'm not out there. I told them all that I miss the street, which I do. I miss working the street. And they just say, "You're a damn fool for saying that."

In one instance the chief of police decided he need not follow a court ruling on how he dealt with the officers under his command: "The federation took the chief to court and got a ruling. He disregarded it. There seems to be a lot of combativeness. I see very little where the administration has stood up for the officers themselves."

UNFAIR OR UNEQUAL TREATMENT

You may see hard work *not* paying off and the officers who cause trouble getting the best treatment.

One officer reported that in his department most patrol officers worked rotating shifts, but a few choice jobs were straight day shift with every weekend and holiday off. He applied for one such job, but even though he had never been in trouble and, in fact, had an excellent work record, the job went to someone else. That someone else was an officer who was getting so many internal affairs complaints, the administration thought it important to get him off the street. The exemplary officer learned that his administration valued hard work less than it valued lack of trouble.

Officers may also feel they are asked to give more than should be required, and that the additional giving is not appreciated by the administration. In fact, it may not even be recognized by their superiors:

> It is frustrating. And sometimes I feel a little depressed, especially times where I have given and I don't feel like I get back. The lieutenant will call and say, "We need you to work this special detail. Come in on your day off, and we will make it right with you. We will remember."
>
> Then a month later I will need a Saturday off, and it is all forgotten. "No, you can't have it. We have minimums," and all this bullshit. You donate your time. You give the best you've got. And you get very little in return. It's frustrating.

DECISIONS OVERRULED

In most police departments, arrests are reviewed before booking the arrested individual into jail. In countless instances a higher authority, often a patrol sergeant, has overruled decisions made on the street. To initially decide to arrest someone, you must have felt the individual violated some law, but that decision is overruled:

> I've noticed that the law seems to be just kind of a nebulous thing. It really doesn't particularly mean what it says. I'll give you an example. A police officer arrests somebody. This can be thrown out by the city attorney, can be thrown out by the chief of police, or by the judge. I've had numerous arrests thrown out.

When correctional officers make decisions to take especially restrictive actions with inmates, they may find their actions reviewed and their decisions questioned or even overturned by an administrator who is not now working in the cell blocks and perhaps never has.

Review is necessary and does sometime reveal that mistakes have occurred. Nonetheless, non-supportive review also leads to the *perception* that officers' decisions are questionable.

CIVIL SUITS

Civil actions filed against police and correctional officers are becoming more and more frequent. In many cases, this action is encouraged by an administrative policy of "negotiated settlements." This means that rather than pursue the matter and assert that the officer is free of any wrong doing, the municipality decides it is more cost effective to settle. This policy not only opens the door to an increasing number of civil actions, it also leaves officers feeling they have inadequate support from their departments.

. One officer reported that immediately before a jury decision in a civil action against him, his municipality offered the claimant a large settlement. Rather than go to trial, the claimant accepted the settlement and the case was not tried. The officer felt he had done nothing wrong, but it seemed the administration was less sure. In this instance, a juror later told the officer that the entire jury had felt the officer's actions were completely justified. They had planned to give the claimant nothing.

Another officer carried this lack of administrative support one step further: "I can think of several instances where the city council offered to pay the punitive judgment against the particular officer. The administration went to the mayor and asked him to veto the judgment, which he did." So the officer was left to pay the punitive portion of this settlement. A punitive damage is awarded because the jury generally feels the officer's actions involved some malice. But in this case the city council must have thought otherwise to make such an offer.

MIXED MESSAGES

Officers on the street (and even in the cell block) are told by the administration that they are expected to go out and fight crime. You are expected to take proactive measures to ensure that the streets are safe and the citizens are protected in their homes. Correctional officers are told to use whatever legal means are necessary to keep order in the cell block. But this proactive work causes frustration because you take a risk when you work proactively. You fear the administration will not support you in any controversy that may result from your proactive work.

DEPARTMENT POLICY

You are probably governed by a thick policy manual spelling out in great detail how to respond to specific incidents. But you are also told you have discretionary powers. Nonetheless, a violation of any section of the manual is grounds for disciplinary action. Consequently, the administration has stripped your discretionary power. It's up to you to figure out which areas these are: "There is a million ways you can mess up this job. You've got a rule book that is two inches thick. All they have to do is wait for you to screw up."

ADMINISTRATION SEEN AS ADVERSARY

Many officers perceive an adversarial relationship with administration. This is worse if you are involved in organizations to protect officers from unfair labor practices.

I always tried to do a really good job at whatever I do. So I get elected to the board, and now I'm in an adversarial position with management. Of course, I try to do a good job. So I tend to get in lots of trouble with management. I am put in a position now where I am expected to be spokesperson and scrapper for people that feel that the department isn't doing right by them. So I am constantly put in a position of caught in the middle, and it really is hard. My attitude is just going down and down.

SECOND-CLASS CITIZENS

When charged with misconduct, officers may feel little administrative support. You may feel you are not given the same rights as those you arrest or control and that the administration fosters a "second class citizenship" status for officers.

Not only are you forced to give statements against yourself, but also your photograph can be released to the news media by administration at any time without your consent.

HIRING STANDARDS

Another area of concern is that agencies may be lowering hiring standards: "I've kind of resented the lowering of police standards over the years to where people are now on the job that probably are not qualified to do police work, but yet through affirmative action have been put on the department." While the administration may be required to hire protected class individuals, you may feel inadequate efforts are being made to find qualified candidates: "They'll hire anybody now if they've got one arm and one good eye." This is a great concern because your personal safety may depend on the competence of the officers you work with.

High turnover rates among prison employees may well exaggerate the perception of lowered hiring standards. It would seem to a veteran officer, however, that many replacements lack competence.

DIFFERING GOALS

Frequently rank-and-file officers see the administration as having different goals than they do. Officers may perceive that while they deal with people's pain, the administration deals with politicians. While officers are trying to save lives, the administration is trying to save dollars. On some occasions it may appear that the administration alienates you from the community through a change in administrative procedure or something the chief or warden says.

> Not to harp on our chief, but sometimes he says some things that make me crazy. Like when he gives a speech and refers to us as an "army of occupation." It just makes me nuts.

MISCOMMUNICATION

The administration may also cause conflict between the officers and the community through miscommunication. The administration may tell you one thing and citizens or inmates another.   For example, most police departments tell citizens that patrol officers will watch their homes while they are on vacation. All too often, however, the inefficiency of the system gets this information to patrol officers too late. Either the home has been broken into and the people who live there wonder why the officers did not watch it closer, or they return and see the officer on the street telling him to cancel the "house watch."

The administrative system may also cause frustration through the court notification procedure. You are sometimes informed of a court appearance a day or two *after* the scheduled date. If you do not appear, the charges against the defendant are dismissed. After having arrested, transported, and booked a suspect and written the required reports, it is very frustrating to see the charges dismissed as a result of bureaucratic inefficiency.

If, on the other hand, the individual charged does not appear, you are required to sit and wait for hours until a new court date can be scheduled. Bail is seldom revoked in this case, and the only person inconvenienced is you for having wasted the morning waiting, possibly on your day off.

TRANSFERS

Larger agencies offer numerous examples of officers sent to schools in particular fields of expertise only to find on their return, or shortly after, they have been transferred. The distinct impression one often gets is that management "just doesn't care":

Another example of apparent lack of administrative concern is punitive transfers. It is well known that you should never tell anyone you are happy working your present assignment. The administrative feeling seems to be that officers should not enjoy their work. Happy officers should be transferred.

> Management, particularly under the administration we're under right now, just totally disregards morale. They use transfers as a punishment, for example. Transfers could be used to enhance morale.

LACK OF INPUT

Finally, most officers feel they have little or no input in decision making. Even in areas where you have expertise or significant experience, you are often excluded from the decision-making process. Your suggestions are most often disregarded, yet it is you who has to carry out the decisions in most instances. You may find this extremely frustrating, a waste of time, and counterproductive:

> It's tough to get up enthusiasm for recreating the wheel. And I watch these young kids become deputy chief. We've had two now in the last three years, and we recreate the wheel again. Here they come, all enthusiastic and fresh with a new idea that we've tried three or four times in the last two decades. And it's hard to gear yourself up, and you say, "Hey, wait a minute. This works, but this part of it might not." But they're not about to listen because it's their baby that they're creating. It feels sometimes like you're shunted aside.
>
> With experience you learn just how important the relationships between people are and that you can't put a square peg in a round hole. You begin, I think, as you get older, to put increasing emphasis on putting people together whose chemistry matches and get maximum efficiency out of people, and to hell with the system, the computers, the files, the cards, and that stuff.
>
> If people get along and you get a good, happy working environment, that seems to work a hell of a lot better than anything else we've come up with. That's awful tough to convince management. They could give a shit less, particularly top management.

SUMMARY

Police and correctional officers often perceive they are separate from management and at odds with their policies and procedures. You feel management *should* be on your side, but too often isn't:

> I guess you expect problems from people out in the street that don't know any better. You can't expect too much from them. But the biggest frustrations come from the inside, where you just have to kind of go out in your car and say, "Forget it. I don't want any part of it."

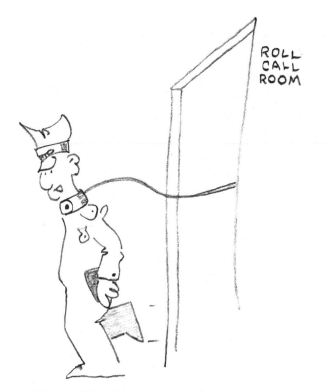

"Seems like these leashes keep getting
shorter and shorter."

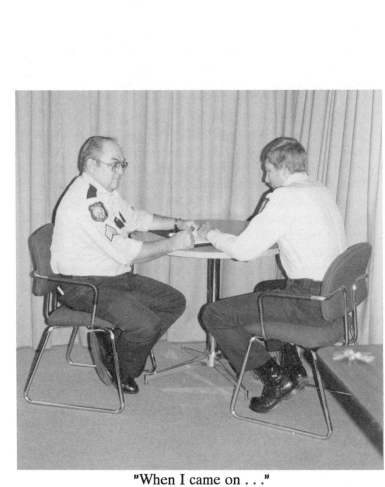

"When I came on . . ."

Chapter 15

TRAINING and SUPERVISION ISSUES

What I really needed was to find out that I wasn't unique, and I needed to find out that it was okay not to be tough and rock hard inside. It was okay to be soft. It was okay to lighten up. We need to remember where we came from, what we were before we were cops, and be human beings.

Being a police officer or correctional officer involves change. This change is often subtle, yet powerful, and can become extremely damaging personally. To lessen the effects of this transition, these changes must be addressed through training and supervision.

You need to learn what is likely to happen, what influences you will be subjected to, and what some common effects are. You also need supervisors who can work within this framework of change to help you be more productive *and* more emotionally healthy. This is the *intellectual* component.

WHAT CHANGES TO EXPECT

Training to make you aware of such issues as loneliness, cynicism, sadness, isolation, and tendencies toward a strong identification with your occupational group must begin *before* you hit the streets as a rookie police officer or begin working with inmates in cell blocks. You must be made aware of what your work really involves. You must understand that you will not always be liked. In fact, you may frequently be disliked.

Your social life will change because of your occupational choice. You will probably not see the friends you see now, unless they, too, are officers. Chances are you will be divorced at least once.

It becomes extremely important for trainers to realize that their training may be accepted in several different ways and that several problems make training in this area difficult. Trainers will find that new officers listen, accepting what they hear on an intellectual level, but still working from a personal or emotional level believing, "It won't happen to me."

Training is difficult because the issues are so expansive. As a new officer, you are asked to realize that *your whole world will change.* At this point, because you have not seen such change, nor have you seen the effects of such change, it is difficult to believe it is really going to happen or be that all-encompassing. You are unlikely to accept these warnings on a personal level early in your career. Having the basic knowledge that such changes do happen, however, will better prepare you for when the changes actually start occurring.

WHEN AND HOW TO TRAIN

The needed training can be carried out in many ways. Police officer candidates can be told of the potential changes during course work *before* the police academy. For correctional officers this training may take place as part of a formal or informal training program before they start the job. Several states require formal pre-employment training for police and corrections officers. During this training, efforts can be made to show officers the potential changes.

Ride-Along Experience. For example, potential police officers may be exposed to "real" police work through *ride-along experiences.* If this is done more than once, candidates are likely to get a more comprehensive picture of what a law enforcement career involves. An individual interested in a career in corrections may spend some time with officers to get a sense of the job.

When you see officers dealing with tragedy night after night, or when you see that some people really do not like police or correctional officers, or even when you see officers routinely lied to, you will begin to get a better understanding of what police or corrections work involves. It is difficult for officer candidates to comprehend the adversarial relationship between officers and those they serve.

Veteran Officer Panel. Another way to expose new officers to what they are getting into and to help them see the potential problems they may become involved with is to use a panel of veteran officers who have experienced difficulties *and* are able to talk about them. These veteran officers can tell new recruits about personal pain in realistic, personal ways. They can highlight that "it does happen to me."

After describing the problems they've had, the officers can talk about the steps they took to resolve the problems and what that change has really meant for them. Finally, they can serve as a resource for new officers *after* training.

THE PROCESS OF BECOMING AN OFFICER

Potential police and correctional officers are civilians. They cannot understand the job any better than others who are not involved and have never done this work before:

> You can't know this job until you've done it, until you've lived it, touched it, and even smelled it. It's not what I expected, and I don't think I could even tell someone what it is really like. There's the war stories and the jokes, but there's a lot more to it than that.

These experiences become part of a process during which you move from the naive view of a civilian, to an adjustment in which you understand the importance of your work but are no longer attached only to your occupational culture. You find value in helping those whom you *can* help and do not senselessly "beat your head against the wall" in frustration over those you cannot help.

Problems of Educational Format. Using only an educational format to reduce the shock of these transitions has several difficulties.   First, initially officers are naive and cannot imagine the realities of the job. By the time you can understand the meanings of a law enforcement or corrections career, you may have already become cynical and hardened.

Once you adopt the negative world view typifying cynical officers, you are too distrusting to believe that your condition can get better through simple education. You have seen too many failures and too many situations for others in which you were unable to make changes for the better. Part of the negative world view is a hopelessness in any real change for the better.

Self-Reliance. Your work teaches you to become self-reliant. This becomes a necessity as more and more police departments are moving to single officer squad cars and prison staffs are becoming smaller. You must be prepared to deal with crisis individually.   Problems develop when you become over-extended and when you isolate yourself from others:

> I don't care if you're working with a partner or not, you're out there doing something and you have to be able to do it by yourself. You have to be able to function. Everything that you do, you have to be able to do as one person, and this becomes a lifestyle.

PEER COUNSELING PROGRAMS

Peers can contribute to early recognition of developing problems for officers and can frequently counsel such officers. This type of counseling can effectively penetrate the walls officers build because it is coming from other officers, people who know what it is *really* like and have *been there*. Peer counseling program officers must be carefully selected and trained.

Counselor Selection. The first criteria in selecting officers to serve as counselors should be desire. All peer counselors must be volunteers because they need to commit additional time and effort to serve effectively in this capacity. Not only will serving as a peer counselor require extra effort, but may require that the officers respond to calls for help at any hour.

The second criteria must be that these officers are not undergoing any severe emotional problems themselves.

Finally, peer counselors must have permission from their commanding officers to take part in the program. If such permission is not granted, administrative problems could hamper the peer counseling process.

Counselor Training Concepts. Peer counselor training should include course work from specific disciplines of psychology and victimology as well as practical work in human relations and communication skills. Officers must learn not only to recognize a crisis, but to intervene in that crisis on a different level than that of a police or correctional officer. They must learn to intervene in crisis as a counselor.

Peer counselors must be trained in family systems, suicide assessment, and alcohol and substance abuse. Each officer can than attend follow-up workshops in such areas as problem-solving skills and referrals.

The officers should also be given a chance (or required) as part of the training, to become involved in group activities where they can get used to self-disclosure and other-disclosure. This will not only help officers become comfortable disclosing information about themselves, but will give them a chance to practice *listening* nonjudgmentally.

Officers should also have extensive training in stress management. They should understand stress and have detailed individual plans to reduce it. Stress reduction plans must include both the physical and emotional components and be *workable*.

It does no good for an officer to decide to run six miles a day to reduce stress if he or she is not physically able, or otherwise can't do so.

The most comprehensive plan, of course, does no good if it is not implemented. Better to limit a plan to deep breathing exercises four times a day if the officer would do that rather than design a comprehensive plan that will never be carried out.

Communication Skills. Each officer's training must also include Communications with a capital "C." This is much more than enabling officers to effectively communicate their instructions. It involves listening, accepting, acknowledging, and respecting the other people involved.

True communication is a two-way dialogue, not just issuing instructions. Too often officers become accustomed to issuing orders at work and then go home and do the same thing.

Implementation. Peer counselors should hold staffing meetings to discuss individual cases and get appropriate feedback from other peer counselors and consulting professionals. This will allow the peer counselors to sharpen their skills while providing the best possible service to their fellow officers.

This must be more than another group of cops or guards who sit around and talk about other cops and guards. More than rumor, innuendo, and gossip are needed. For the program to be effective, counselor-officers need to develop the trust and confidence of the counseled officers.

Accountability and proper supervision for peer counselors is crucial. Each session must be conducted professionally, with consultations and supervision from appropriate professionals. This provides a vehicle for peer counselors' guidance as well as further training. Any individual cases should be discussed without identifying the officers involved if possible.

DAY-TO-DAY SUPERVISION

Day-to-day supervisors can contribute to early recognition of stress in officers and effectively intervene in several ways. Supervisors can counsel you as an "insider," frequently as a "veteran insider," offering suggestions based on past experience and perceptions regarding their experience heightened by advanced training.

Supervisors also can refer you to appropriate professionals, perhaps a psychologist highly attuned to specifics of your work, a peer counselor, a chemical dependency counselor, an employee-assistance counselor, or a marriage and family therapist.

Supervisors must be flexible in their supervision. They cannot effectively supervise recruit officers and fifteen-year veterans the same way. They must blend the qualities of coach, teacher, counselor, leader, and disciplinarian. They must be supportive when appropriate and demanding when necessary. They must know how to get the most productivity from you without personally damaging you. This may seem to be asking a lot of supervisors, but they are in an excellent position to greatly influence the career of every officer.

To supervise effectively, officers must understand the developmental stages an individual progresses through in this type of work. They must understand that new officers may well be shocked by what they see and may not know how to process such events.

Supervisors must also know their subordinates. They must be aware if they are having problems with any area of performance. For example, if they do not understand a portion of the departmental regulations or a portion of the criminal law, the subordinate must be brought up to date. If they are undergoing personal problems that will interfere with their work such as, divorce, serious illness, or a death in the family, assistance must be provided.

Supervisors must consider these problems when making assignments and evaluating personnel. Supervisors must try to reduce or eliminate the impact personal problems may have on job performance.

An Illustration. One supervisor tells the true story of a new officer who responded to a call involving a threatened suicide of a seventeen-year-old boy. The officer arrived and found the boy holding a pistol to his own temple. The officer and boy talked to each other, face to face, about 25-30 feet apart. They began to know each other fairly well. The boy told the officer of his failures, the disappointments he had experienced in life, and the fight he had with his girlfriend. The officer could feel the boy's confusion, feel his pain, and only pray that he would be able to stop the boy from taking his own life.

After the two had talked for about thirty minutes, the boy took a picture of his girlfriend from his pocket, set it where he could see it, put the pistol in his mouth, and pulled the trigger—all in the officer's sight.

This incident posed several problems for the supervisor. First, the new officer had probably never experienced anything like that before. He was confused, blaming himself for the boy's death and not knowing where to go for help. The supervisor had several options in this case.

First, he must assure himself that this incident is not going to place the new officer at risk by not being able to concentrate on the job. Second, he can determine if the officer is all right. Also, he can let the officer know that he did everything that could be done under the circumstances. The supervisor might want to use some older officers under his command to reinforce his own comments to the new officer that he did everything possible in that situation. The supervisor can refer the new officer to the appropriate helping professionals, such as Employee Assistance, a psychologist, or a peer counselor.

SUMMARY

Supervisors must develop reputations as fair and understanding. Officers must be comfortable going to them with problems, and they must work to help solve those problems. Supervisors must not intentionally distance themselves from their subordinates.

Employee counseling is not always listed in the supervisory job description. In fact, supervisors who counsel may be viewed as "soft" or as "strange" by some other supervisors.

Traditionally, little has been done in training officers to deal with these changes or encouraging supervisors to incorporate an awareness of this process into their supervisory practice. Yet this area is crucial to law enforcement and corrections as professions and to you as an individual. Each department must look at these issues and develop a plan to deal with them.

Through training and supervision, the occupational stress effects on individual officers *can* be reduced. This calls for a commitment by the administration not only to train officers in the affective components of their work, but a commitment to train supervisors as well. Through such training, officers will become more productive and healthier. And they will respond better to others in both their professional and personal lives.

"One push of the button on the ACME training compliance unit and I guarantee you'll never screw up again."

Few things work in a vacuum. To help him,
you sometimes need to work with them.

Chapter 16

COUNSELING APPLICATIONS

For cops, the "war" never ends. They are out there twenty-four hours a day, seven days a week to "protect and serve," to fight the criminal–our peacetime enemy. The police officer is expected to be combat-ready at all times while remaining "normal" and socially adaptive away from the job. The psychological toll for many is great, unexpected, and not well understood. Their families and friends have been adversely affected and emotionally wounded as well. (*Williams*, 1987)

Research strongly suggests that police and corrections work is personally destructive and that this personal trauma results in a personality change which may be permanent. This change is troublesome when trying to live a normal life outside work. It interferes with spousal, family, and community relationships.

While tremendous personal liabilities exist, clinicians (doctors who diagnose and treat personality and behavior disorders) find it difficult to work with officers because of the nature of the changes and the system in which they occur. Clinicians must work toward helping individuals adapt and function *within* that system since neither the officers nor the clinicians can likely make any really significant changes.

DIFFICULTIES WORKING WITH OFFICERS

Troubled officers are not likely to admit they have problems, talk about them, or accept suggestions from "outsiders" as to how to deal with the problems.

Denying the Problem. Officers may not understand that they have problems. You work in a system that demands that you shut down your feelings for a time to do the job. You begin to understand that within the system, any real display of affect other than anger and laughter is not appropriate. It is seen as a sign of weakness.

You see others around you working with limited displays of affect (feelings) and perceive this as the norm. You easily translate the lack of display of affect (no show of sensitive emotion) you see in others to a belief that others truly lack emotion and begin denying your own feelings.

You may not admit your problems. Within your occupational culture, problems denote weakness. Weakness is perceived as vulnerability. And vulnerability leads to being hurt by others. It is a risk to admit problems, and you will not take that risk with most people. You will be very careful who you allow into your inner world—who you reveal yourself to.

The police and correctional officers' job is to protect citizens from being hurt by others or to maintain order in a difficult setting. If you do not admit weakness, you are less likely to be hurt by others. Certainly if you can be hurt by others, you are not effectively doing your job. You cannot even protect yourself. It is definitely unacceptable to admit problems to other officers. They don't want to know someone their life may depend on is anything less than capable.

It can be difficult for you to discuss your feelings because you have repressed those feelings and denied their existence for so long. You are not sure you can control them if you let them out. You may genuinely fear that once you open these emotional gates, you will be unable to close them again, or that once you start to talk about them, you won't be able to stop.

Lack of Trust. It is extremely difficult for officers to discuss problems with *outsiders*. Frequently "outsiders" are viewed as the "enemy." You learn, as a key to survival, not to trust "outsiders." Based on that reality, it is inconceivable that you will discuss with such persons, feelings you are not sure you have, are not sure it is all right to have, and know it is not acceptable to talk about.

"Outsiders" are not trusted because you are convinced that they do not understand officers. You start with the premise that "outsiders" cannot understand your work, never having done it. The logical corollary is that they will not understand you or your problems because both are inseparable from the occupation.

CLINICAL INTERVENTIONS

Officers talk with difficulty about their hurts with "insiders" and speak hardly at all to clinical "outsiders." Hence, clinical intervention (attempt to provide psychological help) with this population must emphasize involving "insiders."

Practical applications include Alcoholics Anonymous groups specifically for police or correctional officers, Peer Counseling Programs, Chaplain Programs, and internally staffed Employee Assistance Programs.

Alcoholics Anonymous. Alcoholics Anonymous groups for officers involve troubled officers and peers in self-help programs designed to assist in recovery from alcoholism. A portion of such programs is outreach; that is, officers involved help each other and anyone else who asks them. Once involved, officers see that other officers are helped by the program. They have their testimonials to support what they see and their encouragement to become involved.

Peer Counseling. Another common program is peer counseling. This is a self-help program staffed by non-professionals available to officers daily. This unit is generally staffed to work informally through daily contact as well as on a slightly more formal basis. An officer may be "on call," available twenty-four hours, to handle crisis calls from officers. Usually Peer Counseling Programs serve as an informal counseling network or as a referral base for more serious problems.

Chaplains.   Chaplains are generally volunteers from the community who donate time to work with officers.   These chaplains are resources for officers on both professional and personal levels.

Chaplains are available to help you deal with traumatic incidents professionally, for example, to assist you on death notifications, domestic disputes (once it has been determined no further violence will occur), and with persons threatening suicide. Chaplains become an on-call professional resource for you. However, this works only when you know the chaplains and are comfortable with them as individuals.

Chaplains can also serve as a personal resource for you, considered somewhere between a peer and an "outsider." Chaplains shed some of the "outsider" status when you get to know them as individuals. Officers generally will not give chaplains respect simply because of the collars they wear. You give such respect once you get to know them. Therefore, it is crucial to spend time together in non-crisis situations: in the station, riding along on patrol, at the prison, in the gym, or even over coffee.

Employee Assistance Program (EAP).   An internally staffed Employee Assistance Program (EAP) offers several clinical opportunities. Some establish a variety of groups for officers, such as divorce adjustment groups, post-shooting trauma groups, and professional concerns groups.   Each addresses different problems. These groups can meet on an on-going basis (as the divorce adjustment or professional concerns group) or on an as-needed basis (the post-shooting trauma group).

The Employee Assistance Program can also work with individual officers as needed. Once the program is established and has earned a reputation as being "OK," officers may voluntarily begin to use the available services.

Intervention After Traumatic Incidents. Clinical intervention is also needed after involvement in traumatic incidents. Officers involved in traumatic incidents (determined to be so by anyone involved or by a supervisor) should be *mandated* to debrief within twenty-four hours.

This clinical intervention should take place as soon as possible after the incident, *before* you start to process the event internally, so you can get whatever help you need. The clinical debriefing should be mandatory to remove any stigma of weakness or of "not being able to handle" the situation.

If a *group* of officers is exposed to a traumatic event, all involved should be required to report within twenty-four hours for debriefing. If a number of officers were involved, a small group session or even a series of small group sessions would be most useful for such debriefing.

UNDERSTANDING THE CHANGE PROCESS

Treatment goals cannot be established for officers without realizing that officers cannot go back to what they were. You cannot regain the lost innocence or unmake the changes that have taken place. You must, instead, move forward.

Recall the distinct developmental process in becoming a police or correctional officer. A portion of that developmental process involves seeing the world in a specific way, including isolation, cynicism, negativism, and a general disbelief in the potential for positive change.

You are likely to experience the most pain during the phase you identify with "paying the price." During this developmental stage, you are most cynical, most negative, most isolated, and most pessimistic. As the distance you perceive between yourself and others increases, so does the pain you experience and the need for clinical assistance.

Clinicians treating officers must become very aware of the meanings attached to being a police or correctional officer. They must realize that the changes involved affect every area of the officers' lives. They must understand the importance of the occupation. Finally, they must understand that the cynical outlook and negative world view most often seen, is only one stage in a developmental process rather than an end product.

UNDERSTANDING THE STAGES OF VICTIMIZATION

Many officers' responses are identified in the literature as typical of "victims." Consequently, a therapeutic goal in working with these officers is to help them deal with the pain and to move from the "recoil" stage of victimization into the "reorganization" stage where the victimizing experiences become much less a central feature in their lives.

This probably will mean that work and other officers will become less central as the officers find meaning in their lives away from work. This is difficult because of significant differences they perceive in their world views and those of "others."

UNDERSTANDING PTSD

It is crucial that clinicians working with police and correctional officers thoroughly understand post-traumatic stress disorder (PTSD). Officers may be consistently exposed to traumatic events over a long period.

While the Vietnam war produced many veterans with PTSD, those veterans served in the war for a limited time. Many officers serve twenty-four hours a day for twenty, thirty, or forty years. You never cease being police or correctional officers and can never escape the trauma.

Even when not "on duty," you cannot drive past a traumatic event, a fatal accident, for example, unless other officers are already there.

Clinicians working with officers should be well versed in the research on PTSD in Vietnam veterans. This research provides a large base in that area and shows significant correlation to officers. Both show similar symptoms and require similar interventions.

THE POLICE AND CORRECTIONS ORGANIZATION

Clinicians must also understand the organization and both the formal and informal disciplinary processes. One reward system is promotion. Transfers are also frequently used as a reward system, with those officers *most accepted* getting the reward—not necessarily those most qualified or the hardest working officers.

Frequently those officers who "get along" get the best assignments while those who are more independent work the less desired duties and shifts. This becomes more and more apparent as you rise in the rank structure. The best-liked officers are often given the choice duties. In some cases they are given plain clothes assignments. In others they may be given day jobs, such as community relations, while the rest of the patrol division works rotating shifts.

To work effectively with officers, clinicians must consider all such facets of the officers' world. In addition, this paradigm (model) must include the spouse, family, and community because all are so inter-related. They cannot be dealt with separately.

SPOUSES AND FAMILY

Officers' spouses must be included because officers do not shed the effects of work, the trauma, the antagonism, and the boredom—when they get home.

Spouses must understand the job almost as well as their officer husband or wife. They do not need to know the technicalities, but when you come home and comment about inept prosecutors and crooked judges or problem inmates, spouses need to understand how your perceptions affect you.

Your spouse needs to know what you need when you get home, even though you may be unable to ask for it. And your spouse needs to know (maybe even more importantly) what you do *not* need when you come home from work. Clinicians must facilitate communications between spouses to make these understandings possible.

Clinicians must also serve as resources for spouses. Spouses may be dealing with effects the job has on them. They will be considered a "cop's wife" (or husband) or a "guard's wife" (or husband) with all the attendant stereotypes. They may also have difficulties dealing with their emotions surrounding your occupation. They may be tense or fearful each time you go to work. Spouses, also, may not be able to adjust to the night hours you work.

Most spouses have difficulties related to the occupation itself or the effects it has on you. A major portion of clinicians' involvement with spouses may be education. Your spouse may not understand how the job affects you. You may not be able to adequately explain it. It may be that clinicians can provide this information and show how the job is affecting the marriage.

Your family can have a tremendous impact on you, and your career certainly also affects them. Clinicians must help you relate to your family. Since you frequently place rigid expectations on your children, it is often difficult for the children to meet these expectations. Clinicians must help you set realistic goals and have realistic aspirations for your children.

SUMMARY

It is *crucial* for clinicians who work with police and correctional officers to understand two important aspects: (1) the occupational role, duties, and the impact of each on officers and their families and (2) how officers and families relate to the community and each other. Without such understanding, clinicians will be less helpful than they otherwise would be in dealing with these officers' problems.

"Its my opinion that police officers have little reason for cynicism."

REFERENCES

Williams, Candis. (1987). "Peacetime Combat: Treating and Preventing Delayed Stress Reactions in Police Officers." In Tom Williams. (Ed.). *Post-Traumatic Stress Disorders: A Handbook for Clinicians.* Cincinnati: Disabled American Veterans, (p. 267).

Part IV

PROGRAMS TO REDUCE BURNOUT

This section rounds out the discussion of officers at risk by looking at precise causes of burnout and what can be done to reduce or prevent it.

Specific, practical and effective physical, nutritional, emotional, and psychological suggestions and programs to counteract personal stress are covered. (Chapter 17).

This section includes a discussion of burned-out organizations and how they become that way. Numerous highly productive techniques to reverse the damage and make the organization more effective, efficient, supportive, and less stressful for officers are included (Chapter 18).

Take care of yourself so you can be there for others.

Chapter 17

PREVENTING
PERSONAL BURNOUT

> I just couldn't go on. It seemed that there was nothing inside of
> me to keep me going. I couldn't look at one more dead body,
> one more abused child, or handle one more domestic fight. I'd
> just had it.

Burnout is easier to observe than define. Also, this complex
problem cannot be addressed through a simple formula.
Burnout can, however, be seen as a progressive loss of ideal-
ism, energy, and goals as a direct result of occupational
experiences (job stress). Physical symptoms also may be
present and include headaches, backaches, frequent colds,
ulcers, and sexual problems, to name a few.

High stress levels can be maintained only so long and
then... burnout. Burnout begins when you have been forced
to maintain high stress levels for longer than humanly acceptable. Since stress is the demand on the human organism for
an adaptational change, concern begins when the stress level
exceeds your capacity to respond. An accumulation of
stressors over time can result in a significantly diminished
ability to adapt. The following is a brief review of some key
causes of burnout.

WHY OFFICERS BURN OUT

Some factors making you most susceptible to burnout are:

- Initial naivete and high level of enthusiasm.
- Difficulty in measuring performance.
- Lack of organizational support.
- Poor distribution of resources.
- Necessity of dealing with the public as an adversary.

Naivete and Enthusiasm. You probably began your career with a great deal of naivete and high levels of enthusiasm. When you discover you are not able to do what you set out to do, however, you may have become disillusioned with yourself, others, and the system. The greater the initial naivete and higher the level of enthusiasm at the beginning of your career, the more disillusioned you can become. *You can't burn out if you've never been on fire.*

Inadequate Criteria For Success. In addition, police and correctional work have little, if any, real criteria for measuring performance. One duty of police officers is to prevent crime, but success here is not measurable. Certainly statistics are available, but they tell little about your *individual* effectiveness. They may indicate a reduced crime rate for parts of the jurisdiction, but that drop may be attributed to anything from weather to increased security to changes in reporting requirements. You have little *objective* data on how well you perform your duties.

Correctional officers are required to "maintain order." But what this term means is elusive, open to conjecture, and certainly difficult to measure.

To effectively measure success, you must set realistic goals for yourself. You cannot expect to solve all the crime in the city in one night. You can, however, set a goal of not turning away from a chance to help someone in need or to work more toward stopping flagrant traffic violators.

Correctional officers can also set individual goals. You may decide to work more closely with a particular inmate or to watch the activities of a specific group of inmates more closely. But to set a goal of stopping all intimidation within the prison, for example, is not realistic.

Officers must also focus on their *successes*, not their failures. You must focus on how many criminals you catch or how many violators you stop instead of how many you missed or chastising yourself because you weren't where you "should" have been to prevent a crime or a disturbance.

Further, officers must focus on the process, not the result, remembering that they have done the job no matter what happens from that point on with each arrest made. You must not interpret results *personally*. When the couple who called for help last night because of a domestic fight calls again tonight, it doesn't mean *you* failed.

Organizational Support. Lack of organizational support also contributes to burnout because some officers believe they are fighting crime or maintaining order "alone." Even those in your own department, the ones who could help considerably, may seem disinterested. They sometimes offer little if any help when it really counts.

Resources. Further contributing to the belief that you are fighting the battle alone may be a perceived inefficient or ineffective use of resources. As you see those who could support you assigned to "non-enforcement" positions, such as administrative duties, it may seem that those in control care little whether you personally succeed in your work. This is not to imply that these other functions are not important. The *perception* often is, however, that human resources are not being used to the best advantage.

Citizens as Adversaries. Just as you may feel a lack of support from the administration, you may certainly feel a lack of support from the community. Since the relationship you have with citizens is sometimes adversarial, conflict may arise when you ask for support. Citizens generally want the laws enforced, and order maintained in prisons. However, many are quick to criticize and slow to support those who are hired to accomplish this difficult and sometimes thankless job.

PREVENTING BURNOUT

Officers must develop and use strategies to prevent burnout. Left unchecked, the changes you undergo as a result of exposure to violence, crime, pain, and tragedy can lead to individual burnout.

The symptoms of burnout were discussed earlier as part of the normal development from civilian to officer. You may undergo personality changes that lead you to be cynical, isolated, and bitter. You may see little hope for a "better world" because you see so much pain and tragedy.

To prevent these changes from becoming overwhelming, you must realize this change is normal. You must learn to deal with the job in ways that make it less *personally* damaging. You must take care of yourself. This is the first step in preventing burnout. You must *actively* take care of yourself by developing strategies to do the job without letting the job change your personal life in ways you don't want.

Realistic View of the Job. To begin this plan you must redefine and take stock of your role as a police or correctional officer. You are not there to "save the world." You are there to provide assistance wherever, whenever, and to whomever you can. But you will *not* change the world.

Once you have arrested a criminal and presented a solid case for prosecution, you have done all that is expected of you. If a prosecutor decides not to prosecute, or a judge or jury finds the defendant "not guilty," it is not a personal or professional reflection on you *unless* you allow it to be through either your attitude, beliefs, or actions. You have done your job. If a parole board grants an early release to an inmate you feel is not ready, it is a decision the board must live with. You have done your job.

Some officers may work better under pressure than others and may be better able to handle stressful situations. For example, one officer worked for nine years investigating child abuse cases. Most officers would not be able to do such work for more than six months before it affected them too strongly to continue.   This is accounted for, in part, by how you perceive your surroundings.

Your beliefs become your reality.   When you *perceive* the environment as stressful, it *is* stressful.   One way to make the job easier is to examine how you perceive your work.   You must examine your beliefs.

The "ABC Method" of Analyzing Experiences.   When officers become stressed, they usually claim it is because of an event or experience.   The "ABC method" of analyzing experience shows it to be somewhat more complex:

   "A" = Activating Event
   "B" = Belief System
   "C" = Consequence (stress)

The activating event results in a consequence only after being filtered through your belief system.   For example, if an arrested person is found not guilty, the verdict can become activating event "A."   The defendant's release in itself does not cause stress.   It is the *perception* of what this release means to you that makes it stressful.   If you believe that you have not done your job properly or that the judge or jury didn't believe you and have not done their job properly, that makes the event stressful.   Event (A) processed in light of the belief (B) causes the stress response (C).

Irrational Beliefs.   Edelwich & Brodsky (1980) have identified nine *irrational* beliefs that lead to burnout of people who work in human services, including police and correctional officers:

1. It is a dire necessity for a helping professional to be loved or appreciated by every client.
2. You must always enjoy the favor of your supervisor.
3. You must be thoroughly competent and successful in doing your job if you are to consider yourself worthwhile.
4. Anyone who disagrees with your ideas and methods is "bad" and becomes an opponent to be scorned, rejected, or anathematized [cursed].
5. You should become very upset over clients' problems

and failings.

6. It is awful and catastrophic when clients and the institution do not behave as you would like them to.

7. Your unhappiness is caused by clients or the institution and you have little or no ability to control your emotional reactions.

8. Until clients and the institution straighten themselves out and do what is right, you have no responsibility to do what is right yourself.

9. There is invariably a right, precise, and perfect solution to human problems, and it is catastrophic if that solution is not found.

If you will examine these irrational beliefs, see which are true for you, and change those beliefs, you are much less likely to experience burnout. If you become upset when a person you have arrested is released, you may be subscribing to several of these irrational beliefs. The following is an illustration of an ABC analysis:

Activating Event (A): An individual you arrested is released.

Consequence (C): You experience anger, frustration, and stress, feeling little cooperation from others in the criminal justice system. You question your own competence and relate that doubt to your self-esteem. You may label the judge or jury as "bad" because they do not agree with your ideas. You may find it "awful" that the institution has not behaved as you would like. And finally, your frustration may be caused by the actions of others.

To understand this reaction, look at the beliefs that shape the response:

Belief System (B): The response is filtered through the following irrational beliefs:

- I must be thoroughly competent and successful in doing my job if I am to consider myself worthwhile.
- Anyone who disagrees with my ideas and methods is "bad" and becomes an opponent.

- It is awful, catastrophic when clients and the institution do not behave as I want them to.
- My unhappiness is caused by clients or the institution.
- I have little or no control over my emotional reactions.

The same scenario can be played for correctional officers. If you see the same individual manipulating the system and getting whatever he or she wants in the cell block, it is not the individual's actions that *directly* creates stress. These actions are the activating event (A). Stress, frustration, and anger are the consequences (C), of the action and are the result of the belief system (B), through which the activating event is perceived. Again, using the ABC model:

Activating Event (A): An individual is able to manipulate the system and get whatever he or she wants even though that person is in a penal institution.

Consequence (C): The officer is frustrated in his or her attempts to stop this individual from manipulating the system for personal gain and feels frustration, anger, and perhaps a sense of personal ineptitude.

Belief System (B): Some irrational beliefs shaping the response to this situation are:

- I must always enjoy the favor of my supervisor.
- I must be thoroughly competent and successful in doing my job if I am to consider myself worthwhile.
- It is awful, catastrophic when clients and the institution do not behave as I want them to.
- My unhappiness is caused by clients or the institution.
- I have little or no control over my emotional reactions.

It is crucial to understand that these irrational beliefs will lead to frustration in your personal and professional life.

PREVENTING STRESS

You must also accept the reality of your situation. As a prayer from Alcoholics Anonymous says: "God grant me the serenity to accept the things I cannot change, the courage to change those I can, and the wisdom to know the difference."

One thing you cannot change is that people frequently want "band-aid" solutions for long-standing, deeply ingrained patterns of self-destructive behavior. You may want to provide a longer-term solution, but the people involved may be unwilling to accept it.

For example, as a police officer, you may frequently intervene in domestic disputes and provide the woman with information on how to protect herself from an abusive relationship on a more permanent basis. All too often you find that she only wants the man taken away for one night.

As a correctional officer, you may tell an inmate how to protect himself or herself from others in the institution who want to take advantage of them only to find they have chosen not to follow through on your suggestions and have been taken advantage of as a result.

You may feel that the administration makes decisions that *seem* to be based on misinformation, lack of concern, or simple favoritism. As you find the rules and policies resulting from these decisions stressful, it is important to remember that you may be able to provide more accurate information to the administration. Should they choose to ignore that information, you have done all that you can do. At that point you must realize you cannot change the rules or the policy even though you disagree with them.

Accepting the "Givens." Accept the "givens," understand them as best you can, and work within that framework. It is *not* realistic to believe that all stress can be removed from police or correctional activity. You can, however, work to prevent an *accumulation* of stress in three main areas:

- Physical considerations
- Nutritional aspects
- Emotional and psychological factors

Problems in each area can add to stress and contribute to burnout. Conversely, positive attention to each area can greatly reduce stress and the likelihood of burnout.

Physical Considerations. Stress has been described as a physical response to anticipated danger resulting in a "fight or flight syndrome." In modern society you are often unable to respond to stressful events either by fighting or running. Yet the body is keyed up, ready to go. This tension must be released or, like a clock too tightly wound, it will not work properly and may even break.

Good physical condition is extremely important. As you know, much of police work is done from a sitting position. You are either sitting in a patrol car, behind a desk, or maybe in a restaurant. A sudden demand for high energy output required to chase a fleeing suspect or subdue someone who resists arrest, places an incredible strain on your body. The energy demand may even involve a life-or-death situation. Even if the situation is not that serious, if you're not in decent physical condition, you may find yourself at the mercy of the person you are chasing or arresting. That, in itself, can be terribly stressful.

The correctional officer is in much the same position as the police officer. Just because you are not always in the midst of an inmate riot doesn't mean you will not be in that position tomorrow. Just because you are not breaking up a fight between inmates now, doesn't mean you won't be in the next few minutes.

Again, it is important to maintain good physical condition. The same sudden call for extreme action that can be debilitating for police officers is no less debilitating for correctional officers. Two general areas of physical intervention to reduce stress are anaerobic and aerobic exercise.

Anaerobic Exercise. Anaerobic means "without oxygen." Anaerobic exercise helps you burn off excess tension through activities such as calisthenics or lifting weights. Anaerobic exercise helps build muscle and rid the body of fatty tissue. Anaerobic exercise allows the body to release tension through muscular exertion and can be used in many different ways as a stress management technique.

A number of different exercises affect different parts of the body in different ways. There are exercises for the legs, the back, the chest, the arms, the neck, and so on.

These workouts allow you to reduce the physical tension created by stress. The muscles are worked to the point of exhaustion and become stronger in preparation for the next time you encounter stress.

Aerobic Exercise. Aerobic ("with oxygen") exercise also helps the body to reduce tension created by stress. During aerobic exercise a target heart rate is established and you work to maintain that target heart rate for at least twenty minutes. This is done by engaging in such activities as running, circuit training (see below), cross-country skiing, or even competitive sports.

Running. As a beginning runner, you may start out walking and slowly progress to running three to six or more miles a day. The rule of thumb is to increase speed and distance gradually--no more than about 10 percent a week. You can run as an aerobic workout in a variety of ways. You can run outside, no matter what the weather, run on tracks at health clubs, or on treadmills.

Circuit training. This combines a strength building anaerobic workout with a cardiovascular enhancing aerobic workout. In such training, you develop a "circuit" or routine you eventually repeat two or three times for forty-five minutes to an hour. The circuit generally consists of anaerobic exercises for each part of the body with an aerobic exercise between each. You might, for example, perform a weight-lifting exercise followed by an aerobic exercise such as bicycling and then another weight-lifting exercise.

Cross-country skiing. This is a beneficial aerobic exercise because little stress is placed on the joints and tendons, but the muscles are worked hard. Many gyms are equipped with cross-country ski machines. Home models are also available.

Competitive sports. A sport such as tennis, also provides aerobic benefits. If you can participate in competitive sports without the competition adding significantly to your stress level, the exercise can be beneficial.

Advantages and Disadvantages of Physical Exercise. Research has proven that, in addition to strengthening the cardiovascular system, continued aerobic exercise can produce chemical changes in the brain during which endorphins are released. This chemical change causes feelings of elation and happiness. It also reduces stress.

A final benefit produced by exercise is that as your body becomes involved in a repetitious task for an extended period, stress or tension seems to fade away. The disadvantages to physical stress reduction are the potential for injury, the equipment sometimes needed, and the time required. It is important to check with your personal physician before beginning any strenuous exercise program.

While running requires little more than a pair of tennis shoes and a place to run, weight training can require more elaborate setups. Memberships in athletic clubs are also relatively expensive.

Finally, consistent physical exercise requires a time commitment of two to three hours a week. Although this does not seem like much, you may find it difficult to schedule or may use time as an excuse not to workout.

Nutritional Aspects. Nutritional intake *is* important in controlling stress. Diet changes can reduce stress. You can reduce tension by eating less refined sugars, drinking less coffee, cola, or alcohol, and consuming less fat. Each of these foods and drinks contributes to maintaining a high level of anxiety. Coffee and donuts are not the ideal dinner, nor are fast foods eaten on the run.

What and How You Eat. Instead of high levels of caffeine, sugar, and fat, eat a variety of foods with sound nutritional value. To help control what you eat, use the following "Ten Commandments" of eating as a start:

1. Take control of your eating habits.
2. Eat only when you are hungry.
3. Eat three meals a day.

4. Serve and eat one portion at a time.
5. Eat slowly. Set your fork down between bites.
6. Avoid fatty foods.
7. Do not do anything else while eating.
8. Do not feel that you *must* clean your plate.
9. Wait five minutes before taking a second helping.
10. Do not snack between meals.

A *balanced* diet will help you control your weight as well as your stress level. The balanced diet should consist of no more than 30 percent fat, 55-60 percent carbohydrate, and 10-15 percent protein. This translates into about 87 grams (3 ounces) of fat, 390 grams (14 ounces) of carbohydrates, and 56 grams (2 ounces) of protein for an adult male between age 23 and 50.

Losing Weight. Before planning to lose a great deal of weight or starting a program of vigorous exercise, have a complete checkup and get your physician's approval. Your doctor may have some reasons for you to begin your exercise program in a specific way or for you to begin a specific diet because of your individual nutritional needs.

Don't expect *immediate results*. Learn to make nutritional changes a matter of habit instead of a daily struggle. Take the time initially to look at what you do eat. How nutritionally aware are you? Spend a few minutes writing down what you eat each day. This will let you spend time after a few days looking at exactly what kind of fuel is going into your nutritional furnace.

Some examples of things you might be doing to burn calories on the job are (Violanti, 1985, p.58):

Work Activity	Calories Used
Sitting in a patrol car or at a desk.	760 calories per 8 hours
Driving patrol car.	640 calories per 6 hours
Standing at front desk.	150 calories per hour

This means that for an average shift you burn 760 calories doing routine work. If you are moving around a lot, you might add another 400 to 500 calories burned. If you are not careful, however, your caloric intake may well exceed 2,000 to 3,000 without your even being aware of it.

Fast foods, pastries, and sweets are loaded with "empty calories." Instead, try to substitute fresh fruits and vegetables as snacks. Substitute salads made with green leafy vegetables for high fat meals. Eat lighter and know what you are going to order before you go into a restaurant. The restaurant menu is designed to make foods look attractive. If you spend a lot of time looking at the menu, you are much more likely to tell the waitress to "add an order of fries or onion rings," when you really don't need them.

Stop and think about it. How do you feel after you eat a big meal? If you are full to the point of discomfort, it is unhealthy. Imagine that feeling and then think of how your body will respond to a demand for sudden strenuous physical activity in this condition. It is possible that you might get sick and vomit (hardly a sign of professionalism), or you may cramp and physically injure yourself.

If you eat regularly scheduled meals, you will find yourself much less likely to be snacking on junk food. Even though it is difficult to eat right, sometimes it is helpful to tell yourself that if you can't eat healthy, you'll wait until you get home. You need to decide if you are going to "wait" or "weight."

Frequently you may not even be aware of what you are eating. As you walk past a bowl of chips and take a handful, it doesn't seem like much. But stop to think that you may have walked past that bowl of chips five or six times and taken a handful each trip. Or you may snack more than you realize. You may have had three or four candy bars in one day without thinking much about it.

If you are overweight, you place an additional strain on your heart. You are also much more likely to suffer from high blood pressure, risking heart attack and perhaps debilitating injury or death. Watching your diet and regular exercise will help you lose excess weight.

Emotional and Psychological Factors. To reduce the emotional and psychological effects of stress and lessen the likelihood of burnout, all of the following stress reduction methods have been proven very effective.

Walking For Relaxation. This is one of the easiest stress reduction methods. Little equipment is required, there are many physical benefits, and this stress reduction method can easily become part of a life plan no matter what your age or weight. To use walking as a way to reduce the emotional or psychological effects of stress, you must walk at a *leisurely* pace. Simply walk and focus on the rhythm of the walk or enjoy the fresh air or your surroundings.

During this type of walk, reflect on quiet, pleasant images like the sunset, the blue sky, or the outdoors. Use this walking time to separate yourself from the stressful environment, both physically and emotionally.

Initially, it may be difficult to concentrate on positive thoughts. With effort and practice, it becomes easier. Soon it is almost second nature. These walks should begin with whatever distance you are comfortable with and progress to a distance somewhere in the range of two to three miles. Anything shorter on a regular basis does not provide enough time for relaxation.

In addition to walking, a variety of mental stress reduction activities related to meditation can be effective in reducing stress. These include progressive relaxation, visual imagery, and meditation itself, to name a few.

Progressive Relaxation. This technique reduces your overall level of stress. It takes but a few minutes each day and provides temporary relief from stress buildups. Progressive relaxation also makes you aware of your stress centers to let you better monitor the amount of stress you are experiencing at any particular time.

Progressive relaxation usually begins in a controlled setting, but after time may become useful in other settings where you have only a moment or two to relax. To begin, find a quiet place where you can take a comfortable position and are reasonably sure you will not be disturbed for a few minutes.

It is distressing when you are in the middle of the relaxation only to need to stop and answer the phone.

After you are in a comfortable position, begin to relax by focusing on your feet. Imagine the stress flowing from your feet each time you exhale. As your feet become more relaxed, continue this process moving to your ankles. Again, imagine the stress flowing from your body each time you exhale. Imagine the stress flowing from your ankles, through your feet, and out of your body. Continue this process in this way until you have completed relaxation of your entire legs, one portion at a time paying special attention to any place where you may store stress.

When you move to the upper portion of your body, beginning with the muscles in the small of your back, picture the stress flowing up through the shoulders and down the arms, out the fingertips. Continue this process until you have relaxed your entire body. You may want to pay special attention to your back, neck, and shoulders since these areas frequently become tense in response to stress buildup.

After you have completed this relaxation exercise, spend a few minutes in this comfortable, relaxed position before you resume your activities.

Visual Imagery. Visual imagery can be very useful in stress reduction and can be used in conjunction with progressive relaxation. Upon completing the progressive relaxation, imagine yourself in a totally relaxing setting. Some people imagine themselves in a favorite room of the house. Others imagine themselves in the country, at a lake in the woods, or walking along a sandy beach. Sometimes they are alone and sometimes there are animals in the relaxing setting they visualize.

Visual imagery can become a useful tool for relaxation in other settings. For example, when you are experiencing a stressful event (waiting for something to happen), it can be helpful to just picture the relaxing imagery. Another way such visualization can be helpful is to imagine washing away the stress when you wash your face or take a shower. As the water flows over your body, imagine it washing away the stress and tension.

A number of commercial cassette mood tapes are available to help with both progressive relaxation and visual imagery. Some of these tapes contain subliminal messages. A subliminal message is one you will not consciously hear that is mixed in with other vocalizations or with music. This subliminal message is designed to affect your unconscious to facilitate change in your awareness. These messages can relate to relaxation, stress management, or weight loss. This is *not* an easy way out. No tape alone can accomplish these goals. You have to work at it.

Before you purchase such a tape, try to listen to it. If the tape turns out not to be what you thought it would be, you are not likely to use it and will have wasted your money.

Meditation. Meditation is a form of concentration with an emphasis on single-mindedness. One goal of meditation is focus. This single-mindedness and focus can lead to self-discovery and help you identify what is causing stress in your life as well as how you suffer from that stress.

There are two types of meditation. The first form focuses on the inner world. Like progressive relaxation, you focus on yourself. That "self," however, is more than physical. It is more than your name, where you work, or who you associate with. A goal is to discover the "essence" of who you are. This focus takes the emphasis off whatever events have been causing stress. When you are focused on yourself, you cannot worry about what others are doing, thinking, or how they are interacting with you.

The second form of meditation focuses on something in the external world, something outside the self. The object of this focus can be a candle flame, a coin, almost anything. The important thing about external meditation is that the focus must be on the observed object. If the mind starts to wander, it is important to gently bring it back to the object of focus.

Sometimes meditation involves the use of a *mantra* to maintain focus. This mantra may be a short word, usually one syllable. An example of a mantra might be the Sanskrit word *om* which means "one." While meditating, your focus will be passively directed to this mantra. Again, put any stressful experience aside as you continue to passively repeat the mantra over and over.

Whatever method of meditation you choose—whether you focus on yourself, an external object, or use a mantra—it is important to choose a quiet external environment. Before you begin to meditate, do what needs to be done to ensure you will not be disturbed.

After you have dealt with external distractions, begin to eliminate internal distractions. Find a comfortable position and relax. Do not have your feet crossed at the ankles or position your body in any other way that may disrupt the circulatory process. You may want to use the progressive relaxation techniques before meditating.

After you are relaxed and in a comfortable position (not so comfortable you are going to fall asleep), think about quieting your mind. Close your eyes to reduce sensory input, unless you are concentrating on an object. If you are focusing on an object, look only at that object. Concentrate on quieting your mind. Do not think about stressful events you are dealing with. Do not think of the purpose of the meditation (stress reduction, weight loss, etc.). Simply think of quieting your mind.

As you begin to meditate, do not expect immediate success. You must practice meditation to become adept. Try to spend twenty to thirty minutes a day in meditation. If you have only five minutes, then five minutes is better than nothing. Simply experience the feeling of quiet you gain from meditation. It is something you must work towards patiently, not something that can be forced.

Cognitive Restructuring. Another method of stress reduction is called *cognitive restructuring.* Here you actually look at what is stressful and why. For example, you look at your beliefs about a situation, examine those beliefs that cause the stress, and, if possible, change the beliefs. The ABC method of analyzing behavior (see page 213) can be used in this stress reduction method.

None of these techniques will reduce the amount of stress you incur. They *will*, however, help prevent a *buildup* of that

stress by draining off some of what you take in so you do not
reach overload and burnout.

TIME MANAGEMENT AS STRESS MANAGEMENT

Some things you have little or no control over.   For
example, your occupation may force you to respond quickly to
any number of situations one right after the other.   Or you
could even be in the middle of one crisis when another arises.
Imagine yourself running fifteen minutes behind all day. It
becomes incredibly stressful.   When you try to jam fifteen
things into a time frame that holds only ten, you will have
trouble. The following suggestions for time management may
make your life less stressful:

- Get up early enough so you are not rushed in the morning. If you start the day in a hurry, it becomes more
  difficult to take the time you need later to unwind.
- Take time in the morning to eat a good balanced breakfast. If you are working from a solid nutritional base,
  things will seem to go better throughout the day.
- Leave home in plenty of time so you are not rushed
  either going to work or getting ready when you get
  there. If you have a roll call at 0700 and you don't get
  to work until 0659, you have no time to unwind and
  start the day unstressed. It's even worse if you get there
  at about 0710. You have probably yelled silently (or
  maybe not so silently) to the drivers in front of you
  cruising along at ten miles per hour under the speed
  limit in the fast lane. The need for speed creates stress.
- Don't set yourself up to be doing two different things at
  the same time. You will not be able to do either one
  well, and this will create further stress.
- Don't rush from one thing to another if you can help it.
  Try to program "stress breaks" into your day so you can
  take a few moments and just relax. This will help
  reduce the stress that has already accumulated during
  the day.

- Take a few minutes to "leave work at work" at the end of your shift. You don't need to take your work home.

STRESS ASSESSMENT

One method of measuring stress and burnout is through the *Occupational Stress Inventory* (Osipow et al. 1987). This assessment device is divided into three categories: Occupational Roles, Personal Strain, and Personal Resources.

The Occupational Roles section describes how you perceive your work environment. It has six individual scales measuring Role Overload, Role Insufficiency, Role Ambiguity, Role Boundaries, Responsibility, and Physical Environment.

The Personal Strain section describes your perceptions and the effects of the occupational role. It identifies the effects you perceive from your work environment and has four scales: Vocational Strain, Psychological Strain, Interpersonal Strain, and Physical Strain.

The Personal Resources section has four scales to measure the extent to which you use specific methods of stress reduction: Recreation, Self-Care, Support Systems, and Rational Cognitive Coping methods.

The *Occupational Stress Inventory* is an inexpensive, effective instrument to assess individual stress levels, to determine the effects of that stress, and to identify the coping mechanisms used. The instrument identifies individual strengths and weaknesses in coping with stress and in reducing the effects of burnout. It makes an effective beginning in designing an individual stress management program.

Self-Assessment. As a less formal way of measuring the effects of the job, you may want to answer the following twelve questions. This will give some indication of how you deal with stress and help to identify your potential for burnout.

1. Do I still like to go to work?
2. Do I have any interests outside of work?

3. Are *all* my friends police or correctional officers?
4. What do I do when I feel stressed out?
5. Have my relationships changed recently?
6. Does my job affect how I relate to my spouse and children?
7. Do I take time for myself?
8. What do I do when I am alone?
9. How do I feel physically?
10. Is my weight what I would like it to be?
11. Do I get enough sleep?
12. Do I drink more alcohol than I used to?

If the answers to these questions are not what you think they should be, then you should reassess how you perceive the job, what the effects of the job really are, and how these effects can be changed.

STRESS MANAGEMENT AS A LIFESTYLE

Stress management doesn't just happen. To effectively manage stress in your life you must adopt a lifestyle conducive to managing stress. To force yourself to manage stress can become just another stressor. If you force yourself to work out, meditate, or relax, it becomes just one more pile of stress added to what you already have. Therefore, it is important to practice the techniques discussed, but with *patience*. Realize that you may want to work out every day, but sometimes can't. Allow yourself a day off when necessary. If you eat a candy bar or a donut, it's not the end of the world. Allow that, but realize it is something you choose not to do often.

Stress management is taking care of yourself. You can't take care of others unless you take care of yourself first!

"Beats yellin' at the kids."

REFERENCES

Edelwich, Jerry and Archie Brodsky. (1980). *Burnout.* New York: Human Sciences Press.

Osipow, Samuel H. and Arnold R. Spokane. (1987). *Occupational Stress Inventory.* Psychological Assessment Resources, Inc.

Violanti, John M. "Obesity: A Police Health Problem." *Law and Order.* April 1985, p. 58.

Quality circles work in law enforcement, too.

Chapter 18

ORGANIZATIONAL
STRESS MANAGEMENT

> This place sucks. It doesn't take long before you learn that
> there's no point in doing anything because none of it matters
> and nobody appreciates it anyhow.

Stress management within the organization is even more
important in many respects than individual stress management.
To teach individuals to manage stress in an unnecessarily
stressful environment is comparable to providing a patient
with allergy shots without making any attempt to eliminate
exposure to the substance the patient is allergic to.

For any stress management program to work, the organization must examine the role it plays as a causal factor in
creating stress through administrative policies, rules, procedures, and management styles.

One critical organizational issue in stress management is
the relationship between management and the officers on the
street. It is common for those actually doing the "hands on,"
day-to-day work, to feel that they are getting less cooperation
than they deserve from those above them. Sometimes they
even feel they and management are working toward different
ends. If too many officers in an organization feel there is
little point in trying to do the job, the organization becomes
"burned out."

ORGANIZATIONAL BURNOUT

Organizational burnout is defined as a stage of stagnation. It occurs when tasks crucial to the continued existence of the organization are not adequately completed because of stress-related disorders present in a large number of organization members.

One such symptom of organizational burnout is low morale. The organizational mission becomes increasingly closed and lost in a myriad of lesser administrative issues. This is reflected in poor work performance, increased use of sick leave, alcoholism, divorce, psychophysiological disorders, and a dramatic decrease in service to the public. As the impact of organizational stress increases, it becomes increasingly difficult to get the job done. It is especially difficult if you are motivated to remain productive in the face of organizational burnout because it means you are often working contrary to your peers. You will suffer an increasing pressure not to perform at a motivated level. This pressure may be so great you may leave the organization because of an inability to do the job.

Organizational Stressors. Management also has organizational stressors. The police chief and the prison warden are in the middle. They are accountable to their superiors and to those they manage. While officers demand organizational change to make the job easier, managers may find there is not enough money in the budget to make those changes no matter how much they would like to. They may find themselves "handcuffed" by a city council or board of supervisors that do not want changes the officers feel need to be made.

The department head may not be able to reveal the real reasons such resources are lacking and is blamed for the politicians' actions. Line officers are often not aware of the administrations' stressors, and consequently see administrators as adversaries without realizing that in actuality they are fighting their own battles.

FACTORS CONTRIBUTING TO BURNOUT

A number of organizational features such as expectations, conflict, and physical conditions at work cause individual stress and lead to individual burnout and to subsequent organizational burnout. Police administrators must be aware of and examine these issues if they are to reduce organizational stress.

Expectations. Often the organizational mission is vague and undefined. It is impossible to specify what being "successful" is within the organization. With no set criteria, success seems to depend not on performance, but on other factors such as favoritism. While there are few definitive ways to measure police or correctional performance, organizational criteria for evaluation can be established with input from line personnel. It is crucial that you know how your performance will be measured and what the "real" criteria are for promotion.

Kroes, (1983, p.217) has identified the process of advancement itself as stressful. Because law enforcement and correctional officers have limited opportunities for advancement, competition is intense for open positions. Not only must officers prepare themselves for advancement by study, they "may also have to engage in such distasteful pursuits as buttering up the senior-level officer or as has come to be normal in far too many departments, the 'burning' of fellow police officers."

Conflict. Within the "burned out" organization, officers frequently experience a role conflict. The organization may no longer be able to clearly state its function. You may not even know who your immediate superior is. The inevitable informal leaders may assume too much power in the void created by a weak administration. While the official chain of command may indicate that Sergeant Smith is the immediate supervisor, you may know that to get things done, the one to talk to is Officer Jones.

It is important that the official organizational chart match the working organizational chart as closely as possible. While it is important for a chief or warden to be approachable by the officers. It is also important that he oe ahw allow supervisors and mid-managers to make the decisions appropriate to their positions. Otherwise, supervisors and mid-managers are left with no purpose and little job satisfaction. Also, the chief or warden is overwhelmed with responsibilities.

Buildings and Equipment. As an organization becomes progressively burned out, physical conditions at work will also deteriorate. Buildings will not be as well maintained. Equipment provided to officers may be old and rundown or of inferior quality.

Work stations will not be well maintained. They may need paint or carpet, but most often, the buildings are just not clean. Areas for officers to have coffee or write reports may have papers strewn about, dirty coffee cups and ashtrays in abundance, trash baskets overflowing, and a general appearance of disorganization and uncleanliness.

This reflects the organization. There is likely no *esprit de corps*, and, in fact, a general apathy may pervade the organization from upper management to the person at the bottom of the organizational ladder. Just as no one seems to care for the work station, no one cares if the organizational mission is accomplished.

Many agencies with no budgets for new facilities still seem to have comfortable facilities, and the officers feel supported in that work environment. There is a difference between *old* and *rundown*.

In some cases, officers work on their own time to make work conditions or the work environment better. For example, officers may contribute off-duty time to paint or do minor remodeling at work. They may organize a benefit to get needed new equipment. In other words, labor and management pull together to make their work environment better.

In these cases, officers seem to understand that the administration or governing officials have done all they can do to make the police or correctional work environment better. Administration and officers must cooperate. A compromise might be worked out where the agency buys the paint and the officers apply it. However it works, it shows an attitude of cooperation toward a mutually desired end. This attitude is missing in burned out organizations, and both the officers and management must work to re-establish such an environment.

Squad cars. A most obvious statement about the condition of a police organization is the squad car. Squad cars may be in poor condition and some may not be repaired after minor accidents. Police officers responding to calls for service in rundown squad cars will not be viewed as professionals. If the department does not keep the squad cars in a decent state of repair and appearance, officers do not keep them clean.

This becomes a cycle. As the equipment is maintained less and less, officers care less and less about the equipment. This apathy is often reflected in work performance. You not only find that others don't treat you as a professional, but you may also find it difficult to view yourself as a professional.

When correctional officers work in an environment where professionalism does not appear to be the norm, they also find their job much more difficult.

BUREAUCRATIC RED TAPE

Departmental administrative policies and procedures have been consistently identified as contributing to both individual and organizational burnout. When you are overwhelmed by policies and procedures you do not understand and do not see as beneficial to performing your job, you are likely to "give up." You can fight only so long against a system you do not seem to affect.

As line officers see the bureaucracy become more and more entangled, the organization begins to lose the internal energy that moves it toward completing its mission. Line officers perceive that they are spending more and more time on paperwork than actually doing the job. It seems there is a form for this, a form for that, and a form to order more forms.

Reducing Paperwork. As you spend more time filling out forms, you spend less time in direct service, less time answering calls, less time catching criminals, and less time dealing with inmates. As this process expands, it sometimes seems as though the paperwork becomes the goal of the organization rather than a means to accomplish an end.

As the system changes and becomes more complex, there may be a need for more forms. More and more documentation is necessary to justify what the agency is doing. It is crucial, however, that such paperwork be kept to a minimum and the reason for it clearly articulated to line personnel.

Administrators should develop an agency-wide program to eliminate unnecessary forms and paperwork. It might help to establish a policy that forms be reviewed each year by a committee composed of officers from throughout the department to determine if they are still appropriate and useful or should be combined with another form, revised, or eliminated.

An incentive program could be established to reward officers with suggestions for reducing the amount of paperwork they are required to do. If forms can be combined or the number of forms reduced, it is incumbent on the administration to do so.

Further, changes often need to be made in report writing procedures. If you are responsible for writing a report and you understand its function and importance, you are likely to do a better job, making the report more informative and more appropriate.

Reports should be sent only to those who have a use for the information. Frequently reports are circulated throughout the department, and it becomes a "paper war." Enlightened managers do not want to be burdened with reports they do not need to act on or that will be duplicated elsewhere.

In one agency, for example, officers issuing traffic citations for "open container" violations were required to save the can or bottle, pour the liquid into a sealed container, and place both in an evidence locker. Of course, forms were necessary to track the evidence. This entire process often required an additional trip to headquarters and about an hour of extra work for officers.

Recent policy change allows officers to examine the container, note that the container identifies the contents as *beer,* look at the contents to see if it appears to be beer, and dispose of the substance at the scene. Officers then testify that the container identified the contents as *beer,* and it looked and smelled like beer. Prosecution for these offenses has not changed, but the officers are much freer to issue citations for this violation when they know they will not spend an hour doing unnecessary paperwork.

INADEQUATE INPUT

Another organizational feature that can lead to individual and organizational stress is *lack of input* into decision making. This lack of input applies not only to individual police or correctional officers, but often applies to supervisory and mid-management level personnel as well. Burned out organizations become autocratic and make rules for specific issues that often make little or no sense to individual line officers. Not only do they not make sense, they frequently seem arbitrary and counter-productive.

Management styles are typically hierarchical and pyramidal with the chief of police or warden at the top of the pyramid issuing orders. Police and correctional agencies are organized as classic bureaucracies with para-military characteristics.

As is customary within the para-military model, communication is typically very formal, written, and mostly downward. Those least able to make any impact on decision making are the officers in the patrol cars or cell blocks. But they are often those most affected. This leads to frustration and feelings that there is no support or understanding from above.

CAREER DEVELOPMENT

The term *career development* takes on new meanings in many departments. In some agencies, career development has become synonymous with "punitive transfer." Even more stressful than random or punitive transfers, is the lack of appropriate transfers. The organization does not look beyond the eight hours of work to see the price you may be paying on a personal basis for the success of the organization.

Some of the more stressful assignments on a police department include vice and narcotics investigation, investigation of sex crimes, and internal affairs. In a correctional facility the more stressful assignments often involve investigating other officers or extended contact with high-risk inmates.

Yet, if you do a good job and are difficult to replace in such assignments, you are often left there much longer than you should be. You may not ask for a transfer because you do not realize how you are changing or the effect the assignment is having on you. Or you may fear it will hurt your chances for promotion. You perceive that you will be considered as "weak" and not a good candidate for promotion if you ask for a transfer from a high-stress assignment.

Yet true career development is important to police and correctional officers seeking advancement in their chosen careers. Inappropriate career development or a lack of career development causes problems because frequently you find yourself at a disadvantage in promotional exams. You may find you do not have enough supervisory or administrative experience to compete with your peers who have worked in both areas.

Officers now being hired are better educated, culturally diversified, and less willing to accept authority without question. No longer are the majority of new officers drawn from the ranks of military veterans. Today's new officers are more assertive about their needs and rights and more concerned about true career development. These new officers have chosen law enforcement or corrections as a career and have studied to advance in that career. They are less and less likely to be satisfied spending their careers as a patrol officer or as a correctional officer and want advancement within the system.

INADEQUATE ADMINISTRATIVE CONCERN

Many line officers believe the administration *could* do something about stressful conditions if they chose. However, they feel management is so distanced from the line officers they either do not understand what they need or no longer care. This leads to increased distance between officers and the administration because the officers feel the administration is not concerned about their welfare:

> The bullshit comes from the John Q Citizen on the street, from the dirtbags you've got to deal with—that I understand. That's the reality. I don't expect some guy who spent half of his life being a burglar to like me or ever have any kind of relationship with him other than putting him in jail. I mean, I understand that. I expect him to run from me, 'cause that's the way it is. That's the bullshit.
>
> The chickenshit is the stuff I get from my own supervisor, my own chief, or my own deputy chief. And those are the people who are jumping down on my case because they don't like the way I'm doing the job. They stand back and put a hand up and say, "You do it. I'll just watch." That's the part I can't deal with, and I see that getting worse.

Frequently administrative policies overemphasize fixing responsibility to an individual—"someone must be responsible." Frequently this "someone" is the rank-and-file officer who had no input in establishing the policy.

You end up with the least involvement in decision making, but are often most responsible for implementing the decisions. As a result of this focus, you may develop a self-serving, survival-oriented attitude, further contributing to organizational burnout.

LACK OF SUPPORT

At times the administration may feel they cannot support an officer. Frequently these times surround "use of force" incidents or "injured on duty" claims.

Use of Force Incidents. Such incidents are usually very public and may result in civil suits against officers. Because of "vicarious liability" issues, these suits extend beyond the line officers to the chief of police, and perhaps to the mayor and the city itself, or the warden or the commissioner of corrections.

Since the suit involves upper management and city officials, the decision to settle or to try the case is often made by people who weren't there. Again, officers have little voice in the decision making, even though they are the ones most affected by the decisions made.

Rather than respond "after the fact" to such vicarious liability, administrators must learn to address such issues before they become involved in litigation. If there is a training issue, it is important that all officers understand the proper way of doing what needs to be done. If it is a supervision concern, the issue should be addressed as such. In either case, the concern about improper actions and vicarious liability can be addressed *before* it becomes an adversarial issue between line officers and administration.

Injured On Duty Claims. These claims bring forth several reactions from departmental administration. These reactions vary from actively negative reactions where the departmental administration believes the officer to be malingering to an apathetic response indicating that "no one cares."

You may be experiencing legitimate pain, yet get negative reactions from your superior who believes you are malingering. You may be labeled as not having any interest in the department and accused of leaving the real work to your peers. You may be considered lazy and certainly not someone to be promoted.

In *The Onion Field*, Joseph Wambaugh described a situation in which an officer is injured and his partner is killed. This traumatized officer is ostracized by the investigating detective, isolated by fellow officers, and blamed by the administration for his own trauma.

Jacobi (1975, p. 94) has identified a:

. . . quasi-universal feeling of neglect, that no one in the department really cares or "gives a damn" about their predicament of being injured or ill. ("After you put your life on the line ..."), leading to great frustration, disappointment, and bitterness, with increasing internally-felt pressures, thereby, for retirement than for return to work....

He seems to experience little warmth and understanding from his employers. This is not to say that this is the correct interpretation by the injured or ill police officer but it is often what is felt by him. He feels either neglected or harassed, instead of feeling support, warm concern and facilitation.

Traditionally, administrations have dealt with troublesome employees through a variety of means, most of which do not provide long-term solutions to the problems. Troublesome employees have been ignored, transferred, hidden, or fired. Seldom have departments looked to *rehabilitation* to deal with troublesome employees.

Co-worker relations. This factor will vary within burned out organizations. The levels of co-worker support reflect the influence of supervisory behavior and organizational structure. If both supervisors and the organizational behavior are open and honest, co-worker relations will more likely to be open and honest.

If the relationship between supervisors is competitive and back-stabbing, the relationships between co-workers will be the same. If the supervisor or organization is highly competitive, supportive relationships between officers are less likely.

As co-workers close ranks to deal with nonsupportive administrative practices, organizations become more burned out because the disillusionment cycles through this closed group, growing with each pass.

In many cases the group becomes so closed that even spouses and other family members are not permitted to join. For example, the group may hold Christmas parties and not allow members to bring guests, including spouses.

REDUCING ORGANIZATIONAL STRESS

Organizational changes will reduce the amount of stress experienced by officers, thereby lessening organizational effects. The administration can reduce stress for officers in a number of ways, including the following:

- Improve the quality of department supervision.
- Develop career ladders.
- Develop an incentive system.
- Review department policies.

Improve the Quality of Supervision. Line officers must be supervised more appropriately. Traditionally police and corrections supervisors and managers have been drawn from the ranks of police and correctional officers. While trained in line functions, they are often not trained in supervisory and management skills. They are promoted on the basis of their performance as line officers and on promotional exams, not on supervision proficiency.

The transition from line officer to first-line supervisor is the biggest change an individual officer makes within the career. One day they are "one of the boys" and the next day they are "the boss." Line supervisors have the most impact on line officers. They represent the "organization" in the day-to-day agency function.

It is crucial that new supervisors be trained in supervision techniques. Supervisory training should be part of an ongoing supervisory process that emphasizes team building. The initial supervisory training should take place before the officers begin supervisory duties and should have follow-up sessions to keep supervisors' training current.

As supervisors begin performing their tasks, there should be individual meetings so they can discuss the new position with an experienced supervisor, his superior, or an outside consultant. This will give new supervisors a chance to ask questions about day-to-day operations and to help them evaluate their own performance as a supervisor.

Supervisors should be evaluated on the performance of the team they supervise.

Develop Career Ladders. Another way to reduce organizational stress is to develop career ladders. Detailed steps for advancement, training, and experiential requirements, and the duties of each step must be clearly defined.

You need to know what is required for promotion. While promotions are generally competitive, it is important that you know what you must learn or do to compete and feel that such competition is fair. For example, if a reading list is published for a written examination, the questions for that examination must come from that list. If the questions are drawn from other sources, favoritism may be suspected.

The examination should be given to all officers at the same time. If certain officers are allowed special times to take the test, there will be accusations of favoritism. In one instance two sergeants were allowed to take the written examination for lieutenant at an earlier hour than others because of travel and vacation plans. These were the only two sergeants who passed the written test for lieutenant. Favoritism?

Many progressive agencies have developed career paths that recognize the importance of highly developed line skills. These systems do not require you to become a supervisor or administrator to get a pay raise. You are rewarded as a skilled team member and recognized for your valuable, on-going contributions to the organization.

The department must identify any training needs that will facilitate your movement up the career ladder. If administrative skills are to be emphasized, some avenue must be provided for you to attain such skills. If budgets are of concern, you need to be given a chance to learn such skills.

Develop an Incentive System. Departments need to develop incentive systems where each employee can receive both tangible and intangible rewards for performance. Typically, police and correctional agencies provide more than adequate channels for negative feedback. Specific units are designed just to deal with complaints about officers. Yet few such channels exist for positive feedback. You may not see or hear from your supervisor unless you have done something wrong. A call to the chief or warden's office for unknown reasons seldom gives rise to positive feelings.

When you are given negative feedback, you need a constructive component. It does no good to tell you that your work is "terrible." The feedback needs to be specific with recommendations for improvement. Time must be provided for the officer to improve and a date should be set for a follow-up review.

Commendations should not be given on an arbitrary basis. Instead, a committee comprised of officers from various departmental units might determine when commendations should be given and to whom.

In instances where officers have done consistently good work, some means of positive feedback should be devised and provided by the supervisor.

Review Department Policies. Another means to reduce stress is to establish a policy review board that examines current and new policies. Current policies should be reviewed to be sure they still apply and do not conflict with other policies. New policies must be examined to ensure they are appropriate, practical, and do not conflict with existing policies. Policies should also be examined to make sure that whenever possible they provide long-term solutions rather than band-aid solutions to long-term problems.

MANAGEMENT STYLES TO REDUCE STRESS

The agency's overall philosophy must have as a basic tenant: *concern for the employee.* You must work in an environment where you feel appreciated. The para-military model of management too often has used the "carrot and stick" motivation. True *participative* management will go a long way toward reducing organizational stress in law enforcement and corrections organizations. The basic philosophy of the organization must be that officers want to do a good job and that it is management's function to facilitate that. It is a "win-win" situation where decisions are made at the lowest possible level by those closest to the issues.

Hiring and Training. A first step toward creating a positive work environment is the initial hiring and training of officers. Recruits must be taught that the purpose of the training is to "screen in" and train the best possible police and correctional officers. Too often the appearance is that the agency is using the training process to "get rid" of those they "don't like" and that such dismissal has little to do with performance.

One of the first things recruits should be taught is the organizational mission. This goes deeper than instructing new officers in the duties they will be required to perform. It gives an overall flavor for recruits to see how the organization views its role. It tells recruits why the organization exists and also gives guidelines as to how duties will be performed.

A Common Mission. The mission states global priorities for the organization and describes the function within the community. For example, the mission may prioritize the responsibilities of the agency as (1) law enforcement, (2) order maintenance, and (3) community service. This agency is likely to be very different from an agency that sees its priorities as (1) community service and (2) law enforcement. Different duties are likely to take priority. For the correctional officer the different missions may be (1) punishment and (2) rehabilitation or (1) rehabilitation and (2) punishment. Again, a big difference in message is sent to individual officers.

Career Development. Professional concern for each officer can be demonstrated by true career development programs. Each officer's career should be tracked with assignments, time frames, and goals included in the overall package. As you reach the next stage in your career, you should be kept informed and consulted regarding promotional requirements, opportunities, and future plans whenever possible.

Open Communication. Departments should provide opportunities for *meaningful, upward* communication. Upper management must provide a way for employees on the bottom of the ladder to make their needs known. Some techniques identified by Ayres (1990) to facilitate this upward communication include the following:

- **Advisory Groups**: with participants selected from all ranks within the agency. These representatives will meet on a regular basis to discuss current topics of interest and to provide feedback to the agency's upper management.
- **Department Newsletter**: designed to keep personnel better informed of current issues and opportunities within the department.
- **Designated "Devil's Advocate" at Staff Meetings**: who is expected to challenge all issues at the meeting. This must be done with no fear of reprisal.
- **Executive-Employee Breakfast, Lunch or Coffee**: designated for the chief executive to meet with a representative sample of employees on an informal basis.
- **Open Door System**: to provide access for employees to higher level managers if their concerns cannot be addressed at a lower level.
- **Quality Circles**: consisting of a team of employees who share common duties. These employees are brought together voluntarily on company time to discuss and resolve issues that affect their work environment.
- **Suggestion Program**: in which employees can offer suggestions to upper level management to deal with problems within the agency.

ORGANIZATIONAL STRESS MANAGEMENT PROGRAM

The first step in developing a proactive organizational stress management program is to identify potential sources of stress and eliminate as many as possible. Those stressors that cannot be eliminated should be restructured to generate as little stress as possible.

First-line supervisors are *the* individuals who have the strongest affect on individual officer's work environment. They must be trained to recognize stress in employees and to initiate remedial action. The first-line supervisor is responsible for ensuring that the organizational mission is carried out in as stress-free an environment as possible. Supervisors "set the tone" for everyone. If the supervisor is harsh, unfair, and authoritarian, officers will certainly not enjoy coming to work. If the supervisor is fair, impartial, and responsive, officers are much more likely to get greater satisfaction from the job.

CONFIDENTIAL EMPLOYEE COUNSELING

It is the organization's responsibility to establish a framework for employee counseling. Employee counseling can include a Chaplaincy Program, referral to outside mental health professionals, a peer counseling program, or even an internally staffed Employee Assistance Program.

This counseling *must* be confidential. Any concerns about the confidentiality of department-sponsored counseling will be a "kiss of death" for the program whether internal or external. The purpose of counseling should be made clear to individual officers. If it is to be a "fit for duty" evaluation, you need to know that up front. If the counseling is for your benefit, you need to know that your responses and involvement will be held in confidence.

Chaplaincy Programs. The agency can develop a Chaplaincy Program to identify and train interested chaplains throughout the area. They can be trained to understand the departmental mission, the officers' duties, and be encouraged to spend time with the officers while on duty. Chaplains can be a resource to officers both personally and professionally. Once you get to know the chaplain as a person, an individual, you may use the chaplain as a personal resource. Professionally, the chaplain can be of use in death notifications or domestics, or to counsel inmates.

Referral to Outside Professionals. Direct referral to outside mental health professionals can be done in several ways. First, departments can select specific outside mental health professionals and arrange for officers to be treated there confidentially at department expense.   Second, departments can identify mental health professionals who are part of the health program provided by the department and make referrals there. In either case, unless the request is specifically made for an evaluation of the officer's fitness for duty, the counseling will be confidential.

Peer Counseling. The organization can provide training for peer counselors, an organizational framework in which they can ethically help other officers and provide material support when necessary for the program to work. The training can be held either in-house (for larger agencies), or as a group effort for smaller agencies without such resources. The agency must allow officers time to attend the training, even if it means scheduling adjustments while officers are gone.

Employee Assistance Programs.   An   internally   staffed Employee Assistance Program (EAP) is the most expensive of these programs. The EAP may consist of one or two officers with specialized training who work in conjunction with mental health professionals. These officers may provide counseling in accordance with their skills to officers and refer to selected mental health professionals for other problems. This unit can be used to coordinate special groups (AA, Peer Support, Grief, or Relationship) and to assess stress levels within the department. Again, all participation in the program must be in confidence.

Critical Incident Debriefings. Organizational management must also provide an outlet for officers involved in critical incidents. Many agencies not only have provided for critical incident debriefings, but have also made attendance at such debriefings *mandatory*. This allows officers to process their involvement in the traumatic incident at an emotional level without a stigma of "weakness."

"I've noticed lately that you've been far too happy,
so I'm changing your assignment."

REFERENCES

Ayres, Richard M. (1990). *Preventing Law Enforcement Stress: The Organization's Role.* Washington, D.C.: U.S. Department of Justice.

Jacobi, Jerome H. (1975). "Reducing Police Stress: A Psychiatrist's Point of View." In *Job Stress and the Police Officer: Identifying Stress Reduction Techniques.* by Wm. H. Kroes and Joseph J. Hurrell. Washington, D.C.: U.S. Department of Health, Education, and Welfare.

Kroes, Wm. H. (1983). "Command-Level Police Stress." In *Selye's Guide to Stress Research, Volume 2.* Hans Selye (Ed.). New York: Van Nostrand, Reinhold Co., Inc.

EPILOGUE

So why do officers stay in the business when the negatives sometimes seem to outweigh the positives? The following poem, written to describe a police officer's experience saving a child's life, vividly illustrates one reason.

S O M E T I M E S   B L U E
Candace Benyei

It was a warm afternoon in the small town and he was tired
    but the call had come in urgent
    so he stepped on it and the black and white arrived
    ahead of the ambulance.

He found anguish crying over a limp bundle
    small body in tangled brown hair
    an unwritten book met by censored history
    his own lost somewhere down the dim alleys
    along with the passion.

Now suspended in tortured time he watched
    breathless
    the last flicker of life leaving innocence
    with the fragrance of furniture polish.

He felt for the heart beat but found none
    and met Hell for a moment in her mother's eyes.

He began CPR.

She was three or four in a faded blue playsuit
    barely an introduction
    a short experiment too soon reaching a conclusion
    a last chance.

He redoubled his efforts, now feeling
    the blood in his fingers, his body aching
    with the effort of encouraging life
    without breaking it.

She began to respond and as the color returned
    two became alive in her mother's eyes
    as he met them again with soft words of assurance
    now aware in the moment
    of something no longer missing.

It was a warm afternoon in a small town and he was tired
    but as he rounded the corner
    he caught sight of her
    dark hair swinging through another chapter
    as she walked into womanhood.

And he remembered joy.

APPENDIX

THE PRICE THEY PAID: A PHENOMENOLOGICAL STUDY OF POLICE OFFICERS

Dennis L. Conroy
1987

This study looked at police officers' meanings and under-standings of that way-of-being called "victim" as identified in their lives as police officer.

The research was conducted with 25 volunteer police officers from a large, urban, midwestern police department who were of mixed rank, time of service, and gender. A personal, open-ended interview was done to collect data. Each officer, however, responded to the key question: "Would you tell me what price you have paid because you are a police officer?"

Further research was conducted within a prison where correctional officers of mixed gender, rank, and time of service were asked, "Can you tell me what price you have paid to be a correctional officer?"

A qualitative method was used to interpret the interview data and to find general areas identified by police officers as the most "*costly* price they paid." The areas identified were:

- Loss of innocence
- Isolation
- Cynicism and Negativism
- Constricted and Inappropriate Affect
- Loneliness and Sadness
- Importance of the Occupational Job/Family

Each domain was then examined in relation to universal concepts such as "self," "other," "world," "spacial," and "causality."

A response group consisting of ten officers from another urban police department of similar size and composition was used to evaluate the data obtained from the interviewed officers. The response group was also of mixed gender, race, rank, and time of service. Each officer indicated that she or he had "paid" a similar price.

These officers are identified as *victims*, and the manners in which they fill this socio-cultural role are described from the perspective of the individual law enforcement officer. This includes components of suffering and blamelessness, and descriptions of how the officers experience these components.

The study concluded with clinical, training and supervision, and social implications and applications of the research.

GLOSSARY

adrenalin rush: feeling of excitement and super strength resulting from release of chemicals from the adrenal glands.

aerobic exercise: literally means "with oxygen." Concentrates on establishing and maintaining a target heart rate for at least twenty minutes through such activities as running, cross-country skiing, circuit training, or competitive sports.

affect: feelings or emotions. See *constricted affect*.

alarm stage: first stage in a police career (0-5 years), where officers experience "real" police work and become confused and uncertain about skills needed to succeed.

anaerobic exercise: literally means "without oxygen." Helps build muscle and rid the body of fatty tissue. Includes such activities as calisthenics and lifting weights.

automatic stress reaction: the body's physical response to perceived stress: pupils enlarge, mouth becomes dry, windpipes expand, breathing increases, sweat glands are stimulated, and adrenalin is released, preparing the body for "flight or fight."

beat: specific area an officer is assigned to patrol, on foot or in a squad car.

beat cop: officer who patrols a specific area on foot and gets to know the people in that area on a personal level.

black humor: making light of tragedy to conceal the pain. Also referred to as *gallows humor*.

burnout: a depletion of personal resources, physical or emotional exhaustion, loss of concern or feelings for the job or those served.

Cassandra: figure in Greek mythology who had the gift of prophecy, but was cursed so that her prophecies, although true, were never believed.

circuit training: combines strength-building anaerobic exercise

255

with a cardiovascular enhancing aerobic workout. A "circuit" generally consists of anaerobic exercises for each part of the body with an aerobic exercise between each. You develop a "circuit" or routine you eventually repeat two or three times during a forty-five minute period.

cognitive restructuring: conscious thought about a situation to identify stressors and to try to change perception, thereby reducing the stress resulting from the situation.

command presence: assuming a physical and verbal stance that conveys authority and control.

constricted affect: inability or unwillingness to display a full range of emotion.

curse of Cassandra: see *Cassandra*.

cynical: unbelieving, an outlook emphasizing failure and a lack of hope for change for the better.

cynicism: unbelieving, feelings emphasizing failure and lack of hope for a change for the better.

D - E

Damocles: a member of a royal court who was forced to sit at a banquet under a sword suspended by a single hair to illustrate the precarious nature of the king's fortunes. See *Sword of Damocles*.

disenchantment stage: second stage in the police career (6-13 years), officers cope with job-stress by adopting an outlook of distrust, suspiciousness, cynicism, and hopelessness.

distancing: shutting oneself off from others.

Employee Assistance Program (EAP): offers a variety of clinical help and counseling groups for divorce adjustment post-shooting trauma, and professional concerns. May b₁ internally staffed, or operated by referrals to outside agencies.

external locus of control: feel controlled by outside influences. In contrast to *internal locus of control*.

F - K

flight or fight syndrome: is the physical reaction of the body to extreme stress. See *automatic stress reaction*.

Garrity Rule: requires police officers to answer allegations of misconduct during an internal affairs investigation or lose their jobs. Fifth Amendment rights do not apply.

impact stage: first stage of victimization where one experiences a numbing, a denial of the experience, then a loss of ego integrity and self-confidence.

internal locus of control: feeling you personally have control over your environment and the role you play. In contrast to *external locus of control.*

introspection stage: final stage in the police career (20 years and over) where officers can look back on early career years without becoming emotionally involved.

John Wayne syndrome: being strong and silent. Don't *ever* cry. Simply suffer in silence.

"Just World" theory: the world is basically fair and people become victims for specific reasons. Precludes the idea of random victimization.

L - N

locus of control: where a person perceives control exists, either internally or externally.

mantra: a word or phrase on which to focus during meditation. The word or phrase is repeated over and over.

mediating variables: circumstances that can increase or decrease stress, for example, social support, locus of control, and ability to use denial.

meditation: a form of concentration with an emphasis on single-mindedness. An exercise in contemplation or reflection.

naive: childlike, innocent, or unsophisticated.

naivety: a state of being childlike, innocent, or unsophisticated.

negative stressor: stress derived from something unpleasant, a threat to safety or happiness.

O - Q

occupational culture: a subculture developed by a specific occupational group. Law enforcement and corrections have a strong subculture, with their own rules, and norms.

organizational burnout: a stage of stagnation that occurs when tasks crucial to the existence of the organization are not adequately completed because of stress-related disorders present in a large number of organization members.

paranoia: suspiciousness of everyone and everything, delusions of persecution, a chronic psychosis.

peer counseling: a self-help program staffed by non-professionals, usually other officers, to work in a para-professional capacity with other officers.

persona: a role a person consciously assumes to present herself or himself as felt to be appropriate.

personalization stage: third stage in the police career (14 to 20 years) where goals shift from police work to personal goals. There is less worry about the demands of the job and less fear of failure.

positive stressor: stress derived from obtaining something wanted, something pleasant, for example getting an award, purchasing a first home, having a baby.

post-traumatic stress disorder (PTSD): development of characteristic symptoms following a psychologically traumatic event or experience. Symptoms include re-experiencing of the trauma and a numbing of responsiveness to or reduced involvement with the external world.

primary victim: those directly traumatized, for example a rape or assault victim.

progressive relaxation: a technique through which an individual consciously and systematically concentrates on relieving physical tension.

projection: unconsciously attributing one's own feelings, attitudes, and desires to others.

punitive transfer: changing someone's job assignment or hours as a form of disciplinary punishment.

quality circle: a team of employees who share common duties and who are brought together voluntarily on department time to discuss and resolve issues that affect their jobs.

R - U

rationalization: a self-satisfying but incorrect reason for one's behavior or beliefs.

recoil stage: the second stage of victimization during which the victimizing experience becomes central in the victim's life.

reorganization stage: final stage of victimization in which a person adjusts to the traumatic experience and begins to live a normal life.

repression: holding back, excluding from conscious memory, suppressing.

restricted affect: inability or unwillingness to show a full range or intensity of emotion.

secondary consequences: usually the effects of trauma on other than the victim, for example the effects on the victim's family.

secondary victim: those indirectly affected by trauma, for example, the husband of a rape victim.

special knowledge: the insights into the depth of human experience officers have, but which they feel few others experience.

stereotype: all members of a group are perceived to have identical traits, lacking individuality.

stress: physical, cognitive, and/or emotional response to a situation that is perceived to negatively affect future happiness or security.

stressors: situations that result in stress. May be positive or negative.

survivor's syndrome: concern about staying alive, the means to do so, and/or worthiness to survive.

Sword of Damocles: impending disaster or the constant threat of such disaster. See *Damocles*.

V - Z

verbal force: using a tone of voice and language that convey authority and demand compliance.

victim: one who is harmed or made to suffer against his or her will or without consent.

victimless crime: a crime of morality, prostitution and gambling, for example.

visual imagery: a scene created mentally, generally used as an aid in relaxation therapy, also used to enhance performance.

INDEX

A

"ABC Method" of analyzing experiences, 213-215, 225
abusive language, 18
acceptance, 149
activating event, 213, 214
adaptation, 23, 27
administration, 10, 18, 56, 181
administrative, 27, 28, 177-186
   meanings, 177-186
   policies, 27, 28
   stress, 7
adrenalin rush, 16, 19
adversarial, 81, 188, 210, 211
   relationship, 188, 210, 211
   role, 81
advisory groups, 246
aerobic exercise, 218-219
affect, 48, 79, 131-140, 167, 198
   constricted, 79, 131-140
   inappropriate, 48, 79, 131-141
   lack of, 138-139, 198
   restricted, 48
   substitutes for, 135-138
affection, 76, 167
   parental, 167
age, 27, 44
aggression, 8
ailments, 7, 8
alarm, 24, 41, 42, 43
   reaction, 24
   stage, 41, 42, 43
alcohol, 16, 158, 170, 172, 173
Alcoholics Anonymous, 199
alcoholism, 32, 85, 199
alienation, 9
aloneness, 107
anaerobic exercise, 217-218

anger, 25, 31, 63, 76, 97, 135, 137, 143, 167, 198, 214, 215
antagonistic role, 13
anticipatory grief, 173
anti-social behavior, 45, 46
   victim of, 45, 46
anxiety, 23, 25, 63-64
arrest, power to, 109-110
arresting, 179
attempts to relieve stress, 170
authority, 121
automatic stress reaction, 30-31
autonomic nervous system, 30
avoidance, 9
awareness, 86

B

backaches, 19, 135
balanced diet, 220
barrier to intimacy, 115
behavior, self-destructive, 46
belief, 213-215
   irrational, 213-214
   system, 214-215
black humor, 135, 136-137, 158
blamelessness, 48, 49-50
blanks, mental, 31
blood pressure, high, 19
bringing the job home, 170
buildings, 234-235
bureaucratic, 50, 235-237
burn-out, 31, 209-230, 232, 233-235
   individual plans to prevent, 212-216
   organizational, 232

C

callous, 157

career development, 237-238, 245

career ladders, 243

career stages, 41-45
   alarm, 41
   disenchantment, 41
   introspection, 41
   personalization, 41

change process, 9-10, 201

changes, 3, 4-5, 14-15, 30, 49, 155-157, 161, 187, 197, 212
   personal, 4-5
   personality, 49, 197, 212
   physical, 30
   survival, 14-15

chaplaincy programs, 247

chaplains, 199, 200, 247

children, effects on, 165-170
   lack of parental affection, 167
   lack of parental trust, 167
   parents' special knowledge, 167-168
   problems with peers, 165-167

circuit training, 218

citizens, 49, 103-104, 182, 210, 211
   as adversaries, 210, 211
   second-class, 49, 103-104, 182

civil lawsuits, 102, 180

civilian review board, 108-109

clinical applications, 197-208

clinical interventions, 190-192, 199-201, 247, 248
   Alcoholics Anonymous, 199
   chaplains, 199, 200, 247
   employee assistance program (EAP), 199, 200, 247, 248
   peer counseling, 190-192, 199, 248

clinicians, 197

code of secrecy, 147

cognitive restructuring, 225-226

colleagues, 16

common mission, 245

communication, 171-174, 191, 192, 246
   lack of, 171-174
   with spouses, 171-174

competitive sports, 218-219

concentration, loss of, 31

concern, lack of, 239

confidential employee counseling, 247-248

conflicts, 7, 84, 233-234
   internal, 84
   job, 7

confusion, 31

consequence, 213, 214

constricted affect, 79, 131-140

control, 24, 35-36, 48, 49, 62-63, 72-73, 74, 131-134
   lack of, 24, 48, 49
   locus of, 72-73, 74
   need for, 131-134

coping mechanisms, 158

corrections, 13-20

corrections family, importance of, 141-151

counseling programs, 190-192, 197-208, 247-248
   applications, 197-208
   communication, 192
   implementing, 192
   selecting, 191
   training, 191-192

court battles, 67-68

co-worker relations, 241

crime, victim of, 45-46

crimes of morality, 123

critical incident debriefing, 248

criticism, 7, 107, 108
  public, 7
cross-country skiing, 218
culture, occupational, 142, 189
culture, police, 10
cynical, 15-16, 42, 137, 190, 201
  outlook, 15, 201
cynicism, 9, 10, 15, 42, 72, 79, 85, 95-106, 111, 119, 135, 187, 201

D

dangers, 6, 16, 18, 29, 39, 70, 134, 173
  denial of, 134
  fear of, 173
deadly force, use of, 60
death, fear of, 173-174
deception, 9
defense mechanisms, stress, 9
  avoidance, 9
  deception, 9
  projection, 9
  rationalization, 9
  repression, 9
  substitution, 9
demand, 24-25
  occupational, 24-25
denial, 40, 70, 71, 74, 132-134, 198
  of danger, 134
  of emotions, 132
  of fear, 134
  of pain, 1133
  of personal involvement, 71
  of vulnerability, 133-134
dental problems, 31
department newsletters, 246
departmental response, 50-51
depression, 7, 8, 9, 23, 25-26, 31, 58, 63, 101
despair, 9

developing career ladders, 243
devil's advocate, 246
difficulties working with officers, 197
difficulty, measuring performance, 210-211
disability, employee, 23
disappointment, 97, 99, 111, 114
disaster, natural, 47
disenchantment stage, 41-43
disillusionment, 100-101
disorder, post-traumatic stress, 23, 55-76, 79
disorganization, 31
distance, emotional, 72, 75
distancing, 38, 72, 75, 112, 119
distrust, 7, 15-16, 18, 35, 76, 98, 121, 137, 156, 190
  professional, 35
disturbances, sleep, 63, 65, 71, 72
divorce, 32, 46, 85, 144, 159, 169, 173
do-gooders, 100, 102-103
drinking, 7, 8, 158
drugs, 158

E

educational format, problems of, 190
effects on children, 165-170
egocentric thinking, 25
emotional considerations, 222-226
emotional difficulties, 76
emotional distancing, 72, 75, 112, 119
emotional responses to stress, 31-32
emotional suffering, 48
emotional trauma, 55-76

emotional treadmill, 69
emotional turmoil, 172
emotional unpredictability, 75
emotions, denial of, 132
employee assistance program (EAP), 199, 200, 247, 248
employee disability, 23
enemy, unknown, 56
energy, loss of, 88-89
energy drain, 169-170
enthusiasm, 210
equipment, 234-235
excitement, 7
exercise, 217-219
exhaustion, 24
expectations, 38-39, 233
external factors of loneliness, 107-110
external locus of control, 72-73
extra-marital involvements, 172-173

F
failure, 26
fairness, loss of, 99-104
faith, loss of, 88
families of officers, 203-204
family, 17, 79, 141-151, 203-204
    police/corrections, 141-151
fear, 31, 97, 111, 114, 126-127, 134, 173-174
    denial of, 134
    of being inappropriate, 126, 127
    of danger, 173
    of death, 173-174
    of investing, 111
fight-or-flight syndrome, 30
flashbacks, 58, 71
force, use of, 60, 240
    deadly, 60
forces of nature, victim of, 45, 47
format, educational problems, 190
friends, 16-17
frustration, 111, 157, 177, 214, 215
functioning, personal, 7
futility, 26, 37

G
Garrity Rule, 103
geographic reminders, 66-67
goals, realistic, 210
grief, anticipatory, 173
guilt, 25, 26, 74

H
hazard, professional, 9
headaches, 19, 31
headlines, newspaper, 103
health, 160-161
heart attacks, 19, 31
"helping professionals", 59
helplessness, 26
high blood pressure, 19
hiring, 182, 245
    standards, 182
homelife, 169
    energy drain, 169
    time drain, 169
hopelessness, 24, 26, 42, 190
hormones, 31
hostage, 16, 58
human suffering, 86
humanity, loss of, 91-92
hurt, 97
hyperalertness, 72
hypertension, 135

I
illness, stress related, 31
imagery, visual, 223-224

imbalance, 26
impact, 40, 42, 43
importance of the job, 159
importance of the police/corrections family, 141-151
impression, skewed, 82
improving the quality of supervision, 242-243
inability to talk, 114-115
inability to trust, 35, 110
inadequate support, 177-178
inappropriate, fear of being, 126-127
inappropriate affect, 48, 79, 130-141
inappropriate emotions, 167
incarceration power, 109-110
incentives, 243-244
inferior judgment, 31
informal rules, 142
injured on duty, 240-241
injustice, 100
innocence, loss of, 15-16, 50, 79, 81-94, 112, 125, 156
input, lack of, 184, 237
insufficient resources, 210, 211
integrity, 104
interest in work, loss of, 7-8
internal conflict, 84
internal factors of loneliness, 110-115
internal locus of control, 72-73
interpretation, 72, 74
intervention after traumatic incidents, 200-201
intimacy, 112-113, 114, 115, 137, 138, 171
  barriers to, 115
introspection stage, 41, 43, 44
intrusion, 70, 71
investing, fear of, 111
involvement with strangers,
113-114, 172-173
invulnerability, personal, 60-61
irrational beliefs, 213-214
isolated, 45, 49, 111, 173
isolation, 10, 45, 79, 119-130, 158-159, 187
  physical, 119
  psychological, 119

J
job, realistic view of, 212-213
job conflicts, 7
job perspective, 101-102
job responsibility, 18
judgment, inferior, 31
'Just World" theory, 37
justice, loss of, 99-104

K
key components of victimization, 48-50
  blamelessness, 48, 49-50
  emotional suffering, 48
  physical suffering, 48
  social suffering, 48
  suffering, 48
knowledge, 87, 111-112, 167-168

L
lack of affect, 138-139
lack of communication with spouses, 171-174
lack of concern, 239
lack of control, 24, 48, 49
lack of input, 184, 237
lack of intimacy, 112-113, 171
lack of organizational support, 210, 211
lack of parental affection, 167
lack of popular support, 56
lack of positive feelings, 61

lack of support, 7, 14, 18, 28,29,
　51, 107, 109, 177-178, 210,
　211, 239-241
lack of trust, 35, 42, 98-99, 121,
　167, 198-199
ladders, career, 243
laughter, 135, 143, 167, 198
lawsuits, civil, 102, 180
liabilities, 197
life-or-death situation, 217
locus of control, 72-73, 74
loneliness, 9, 10, 42, 79, 107-
　118, 187
　external causes of, 107-110
　internal causes of, 110-115
loss, potential, 27
loss of concentration, 31
loss of energy, 88-89
loss of fairness, 99-104
loss of faith, 88
loss of hope, 101
loss of humanity, 91-92
loss of innocence, 15-16, 79,
　81-94, 112, 125, 156
loss of interest in work, 7-8
loss of justice, 99-104
loss of naivety, 15
loss of self-confidence, 89-90
loss of the past, 92, 114
loss of values, 90-91, 99-104
low self-esteem, 32

M
maladaptive behavior, 9
management styles, 244-246
mantra, 224, 225
marital problems, 19, 58, 75-76
McGrath, 23, 24-25
measuring performance, diffi-
　culty of, 210-211
media coverage, 148, 174
mediating variables, 72, 74

meditation, 224-225
memories of trauma, 71
mental blanks, 31
minority group status, 144-147
miscommunication, 182-183
mission, 245
mixed messages, 180-181
models of stress, 23-28, 43
　McGrath, 23, 24-25
　other, 26-27
　Parr, 23, 25-26
　Selye, 23-24
　Violante, 23, 26, 43
morality, 122-123
　crimes of, 123
mortality, 66

N
naivety, 83, 85, 95, 112, 189,
　190, 210
naivety, loss of, 15
nature of the work as a cause
　of isolation, 120-121
nature, victim of, 45, 47
need, 26
need for control, 131-134
negative attitude, 98
negative stressors, 28-30
negativism, 79, 97-98, 104, 190,
　201
new awareness, 86
news stories, 67-68
newsletter, department, 246
newspaper headlines, 103
nightmares, 58, 63, 64-65, 71
numbing, 69
nutritional considerations, 219

O
occupational choice, 165
occupational culture, 142, 189

occupational dangers, 6
occupational demand, 24-25
occupational family, 79, 143-144, 148-151
occupational stress, 170
Occupational Stress Inventory, 227
officer safety, 36
official roles, 123-128
on-the-job disappointments, 99
open communication, 246
open-door system, 246
organizational burnout, 232
organizational issues, 231-249
organizational stress management, 231-249
organizational stressors, 232, 242-244
    reducing, 242-244
organizational support, lack of, 210, 211
outsiders, 198-199
over-protectiveness, 76

P
pain, denial of, 133
panel of veteran officers, 189
paperwork, 7, 51, 235-237
paranoia, 63, 64-65
parental affection, lack of, 167
parental trust, lack of, 167
parents' special knowledge, 167-168
Parr, 23, 25-26,
participative management, 244
past, loss of the, 92, 114
peer counseling programs, 190-192, 199, 248
    communication, 192
    implementing, 192
    selecting, 191
    training, 191-192

peers, problems with, 165-167
perception, 24, 213
perceptions of reality, 125-126
performance, difficulty in measuring, 210-211
personal burnout, preventing, 209-230
personal changes, 4-5
personal disappointments, 99
personal functioning, 7
personal invulnerability, 60, 61
personal liabilities, 197
personal vulnerability, 60-61
personality, 72
personality changes, 49, 197, 212
personalization stage, 41, 43, 44
physical condition, 217-219
physical danger, 29, 39
physical difficulties, 76
physical exercise, advantages and disadvantages, 219
physical injuries, 69
physical isolation, 119
physical power, 145
physical safety, 168
physical suffering, 48
physiological responses, 30
police administrations, 10, 18, 56
police culture, 10
police family, importance of, 141-151
police shootings, 65
policies, 27, 28, 181, 244
    administrative, 27, 28
poor distribution of resources, 210, 211
popular support, lack of, 56
positive feelings, lack of, 61
positive stressors, 28

post-trauma stress, 71, 74-75
post-traumatic stress disorder (PTSD), 23, 55-76, 79, 81, 202
  diagnostic criteria for, 57-58
  two-phase model, 70-71
potential loss, 27
power, 145, 149
power to arrest, 109-110
powerlessness, 18, 61, 62-63, 65
preparedness, 27
preparing for the job, 65-66
pressure, 27
pre-trauma personality, 72
pre-trauma stress, 72
preventing burnout, 209-230
preventing stress, 215-221, 222-226
  emotional/psychological considerations, 222-226
  nutritional considerations, 219
  physical considerations, 219
primary, 59
primary victims, 39-40, 50
problems, 19, 31, 58, 75-76, 165-167, 190, 198
  dental, 31
  marital, 19, 58, 75-76
  stomach, 19
  with peers, 165-167
process, socialization, 44
process of becoming an officer, 189-190
process of change, 9-10, 201
professional distrust, 35
professional duties, 124
professional hazard, 9
"professionals, helping," 59
progressive relaxation, 222-223
projection, 9
promiscuity, 7, 8

protection, 36, 37-38
pseudo-intimacy, 114
psychological considerations, 222-226
psychological isolation, 119
psychological trauma, 37
public criticism, 7
public expectations, 38-39
punitive transfers, 183, 237

Q
quality circles, 246
quality of supervision, 242-243

R
rationalization, 9
reactions, 27, 30, 72, 74
realist, 104
realistic, 104, 212
realistic goals, 210
realities, 132, 147-148, 190, 216
reality, perceptions of, 125-126, 213
reasons for becoming officers, 84-85
reclusiveness, 7, 8
recoil, 40, 41, 42, 43
red tape, 235-237
reducing organizational stress, 242-244
re-experiencing the traumatic event, 67-68, 74
relationships, 188, 231, 241
relaxation, progressive, 222-223
relieving stress, 170
reminders, 65-68
  geographic, 66-67
  responses of other officers, 67
  situational, 65-66
reorganization, 40, 41, 43, 44, 50

repeated exposure to traumatic events, 68-69
repression, 9
reputation, 103-104
resistance, 24
resources, 210, 211
  insufficient, 210, 211
  poor distribution of, 210, 211
responses, 24, 30, 31-32, 67
  emotional, 31-32
  physiological, 30
responsibility, job, 18
restricted affect, 48
re-victimized, 74
ride-alongs, 188
risk, 99, 111, 113, 114, 134, 198
rookie stage, 95-96
rotating schedules, 160
rotating shifts, 29, 160, 169
routine, 18
rules, informal, 142
running, 218

S

sadness, 10, 79, 97, 111, 187
safety, 36, 168
  officer, 36
  physical, 168
schedules, work, 18, 159-161, 168-169
second-class citizens, 49, 103-104, 182
second guessing, 120
secondary, 59
secondary consequences, 74
secondary victims, 39, 40
secrecy, reasons for, 145-147
self, victim of, 45, 46
self-assessment, 227-228
self-care, 36
self-confidence, loss of, 89-90

self-destructive behavior, 46
self-esteem, low, 32
self-image, 150
self-reliance, 190
Selye, 23-24
senselessness, 38
separateness, 145
severe depression, 63
sex, 27, 44
sexual innuendos, 18
shifts, rotating, 29, 160, 169
shooting incident, 66-67
shootings, police, 65
similar call reminders, 66-67
similarities of corrections officers and police officers, 13-14
situational reminders, 65-68
skewed impression, 82
sleep disturbances, 63, 64-65
social life, 123-128
social status, 27, 48-49
social suffering, 48-49
social support, 27, 74
socialization process, 44
special knowledge, 87, 111-112, 167-168
  parents', 167-168
spouses, 171-174, 203-204
squad cars, 120, 235
stage, 40-45
  introspection, 41, 43, 44
  personalization, 41, 43, 44
  victimization, 40-45
stages, career, 41-45
stages of stress, 24
stages of victimization, 40-45, 202
  alarm, 41, 42, 43
  disenchantment, 41, 42, 43
  impact, 40, 42, 43
  introspection, 41, 43, 44
  personalization, 41, 43, 44

recoil, 40, 41, 42, 43
reorganization, 40, 41, 43, 44
standards, hiring, 182
status, social, 27, 48-49, 144-147
stereotypes, 14, 38, 122, 147-148, 161
stomach problems, 19, 31
strangers, involvement with, 113-114
stress, 7, 9, 23-28, 30, 55-76, 79, 170, 191, 202, 216-221, 227-228, 231-249
  administrative, 7
  assessment, 191, 227-228
  defense mechanisms, 9
  management, organizational, 231-249
  management plan, 191, 228, 246-247
  models of, 23-28
  occupational, 170
  post-trauma, 23, 55-76, 79, 202
  pre-trauma, 72, 73
  preventing, 215-221
  reaction, 30
  relieving, 170, 242-244
  theories of, 43
  work, 23
stressors, 27-30, 232
  negative, 28-29
  organizational, 232
  positive, 28
stress-related illness, 31
substitute actions, 137-138
substitutes for affect, 135-138
  anger, 135
  black humor, 135, 136-137
  laughter, 135
  physical, 135

substitute actions, 137-138
substitution, 9, 135-138
suffering, 48-49, 86
  emotional, 48
  physical, 48
  social, 48-49
suggestion programs, 246
suicide, 7, 8, 32, 46, 85, 158
supervision, 187-196, 242-243
supervisors, 18, 192-193
support, 150-151
support, lack of, 7, 14, 18, 28-29, 51, 56, 107, 109, 177-178, 210, 211, 239-241
support, social, 27, 74
surroundings, 27
survival changes, 14-15
survival mechanisms, 99
survivor syndrome, 56, 63
suspicion, 7, 167
Sword of Damocles, 110

T
talk, inability to, 114-115
technology, victim of, 45, 46-47
tension, 18, 27
threat, 18, 27
time drain, 169-170
time management, 226-227
tragedy, 131
training, 39, 187-196, 191-192, 245
transfers, 183, 237
  punitive, 183, 237
transition, 167, 187, 190
trauma, 37, 41, 72-75, 197
  emotional, 41
  psychological, 37
  types of, 72, 73-74
traumatic events, repeated exposure to, 68-69, 202

trust, 15, 35, 98-99, 110, 121, 198-199
  inability to, 110
  lack of, 35, 98-99, 121,198-199
TV cops/guards, 147-148
two-phase model, 70-71
types of trauma, 73-74

U
ulcers, 31
uncontrolled forces of nature, victim of, 45, 47
understaffed, 18
unequal treatment, 178-179
unfairness, 100, 178-179
unknown enemy, 56
unreasonable standards, 165
use of deadly force, 60
use of force, 60, 240
uselessness, 26, 111

V
values, loss of, 90-91, 99-104
veteran officer panel, 189
victimization, 13, 35-51, 79, 202
  key components of, 48-50
  primary vs. secondary, 39
  process of, 41
  stages of, 40-45, 202
victimless crimes, 123
victims, 13, 35-51, 109
  primary, 39
  secondary, 39
vigilance, 7
Violante, 23, 26
violence, 137
visibility, 145
visual imagery, 223-224
vulnerability, 5, 16, 35, 36, 39, 45, 60-61, 91, 131-134, 198
  denial of, 133-134

W
walking, 222
walls, 115-116
weakness, 36, 39, 45, 71, 198, 201
withdrawal, 8, 58, 101, 171
work schedule, 159-161, 168-169
work stress, 23
working model of stress, 27-28